WEST LOTHIAN

Edited by Chris Hallam

First published in Great Britain in 2003 by
YOUNG WRITERS
Remus House,
Coltsfoot Drive,
Peterborough, PE2 9JX
Telephone (01733) 890066

SB ISBN 1 84460 254 0

FOREWORD

Young Writers was established in 1991 as a foundation for promoting the reading and writing of poetry amongst children and young adults. Today it continues this quest and proceeds to nurture and guide the writing talents of today's youth.

From this year's competition Young Writers is proud to present a showcase of the best poetic talent from across the UK. Each hand-picked poem has been carefully chosen from over 66,000 'Hullabaloo!' entries to be published in this, our eleventh primary school series.

This year in particular we have been wholeheartedly impressed with the quality of entries received. The thought, effort, imagination and hard work put into each poem impressed us all and once again the task of editing was a difficult but enjoyable experience.

We hope you are as pleased as we are with the final selection and that you and your family will continue to be entertained with *Hullabaloo! West Lothian* for many years to come.

CONTENTS

Bankton Primary School

Ailsa Stryke (10)	75
Graham Gillies (10)	76
Greg Mann (10)	77
Laura Thomson (11)	78
Toni Cochrane (10)	79
Dean Stephens (11)	79
Kerry Stewart (11)	80
Corey Prigmore (11)	81
Lois Smith (10)	81
Ruth Murray (11)	82
Hannah Brownlie (10)	83
Craig Mahood (10)	84
Rochelle Fagan (10)	85
Connel Thompson (10)	86
Michael Storrie (11)	87
Stacey Noble (9)	87
James Dunn (8)	88
Edward Watt (11)	88
Nicole Hoffie (8)	89
Bethanie Combe (9)	89
Craig Wilson (9)	90
Holly Simpson (10)	90
Lauren Westwood (9)	91
Christopher Little (9)	91
Blair Stryke (8)	92
Beth Hutchison (9)	92
Lisa Brownlie (8)	93
Louise Henderson (11)	93
Lori Nelson (8)	94
Christie Hyde (11)	94
Neil Mann (8)	95
Samantha MacLeod (11)	95
Ashleigh Stephens (8)	96
Christopher Tucker (11)	96
Jack Thompson (8)	97
Ross Fagan (11)	97
Chloe Bartlett (8)	98
Liam Pace (11)	98

Sean Durnan (8)	99
Christopher McGhee (9)	99
Ross Goodfellow (11)	100
Jamie McRoberts (9)	100
Rachael Ralston (11)	101
Michael McCormick (10)	101
Erin Bradley (11)	102
Stephen McCutcheon (9)	102
Stacey Linney (8)	103
Blayre Currie (11)	103
Benjamin Snodgrass (8)	104
Kerry-ann Symington (8)	105
Aaron Galvin (9)	106
Alastair Stirrat (8)	106
Ben Harman (10)	107

Blackridge Primary School

Carrie Burnett (10)	107
Carrie Leighann Boardman (10)	108
Rachel Craig (10)	109

Letham Primary School

Martin Caldwell (10)	110
Scott Bates (11)	110
Daniel McGuckin (11)	111

Springfield Primary School

Leanne Temple (11)	111
Louisa Brown (11)	112
Andrew Cochrane (11)	112
Sarah Litster (11)	112
Lisa Greig (11)	113
Kathryn Swanson (11)	113
Kathryn Nieuwstadt (11)	114
Gillian Scott (11)	114
Hazel McCartney (11)	115
Rachael Doherty (11)	115
Natasha Black (11)	116

Scott Noon (11)	117
Ailie McClay (11)	117
Katie Turnbull (11)	118
Alexander Chadwick (11)	118
Scott Fyfe (11)	119
Ross Shepherd (11)	119
Stuart Grant (11)	120
Kirsten Trayner (10)	120
Lisa Hunter (11)	120
Andrew Blythe (10)	121
Iain Grant (11)	122

Toronto Primary School

Callum Walker (11)	122
Hannah Stirling (11)	123
Rosie Smeaton (11)	124
Aleisha Evans (11)	124
Kirsty Kilfeather (10)	125
Rachel Scoular (11)	126
Saqib Iqbal (11)	127
Christopher Robertson (11)	127
Samantha Wardlaw (11)	128
Naomi Young (11)	128
Dawn Balfour (11)	129

Torphichen Primary School

Duncan Ewing (9)	129
Callum Anderson (9)	130
Richard Bartlett (11)	131
Raina Gillon (10)	132
Emma Thacker (10)	133
Megan Kavanagh (10)	134
Tabitha Ewing (11)	134
Liam Russell (11)	135
Natalie Rigby (10)	136
Imogen Beck (8)	137
Heather Wolfe (8)	138
Alice Gunn (10)	139

The Poems

WINTER

Snow as white as white can be
Ice is really slippery
Wind blows tiles off the roof
Footprints off the animals' feet
Winter is very cold, but fun to play in

Putting the Christmas tree up is really tricky
Making snowmen is really fun
Making snow angels is wet and snowy
Igloos are very tricky to make
Winter is always fun

A warm, woolly scarf round our neck
Blue wellies to keep my feet dry
Woolly hat and gloves to keep my head and hands warm
Woolly socks to keep our feet warm
Winter is when I need my warm clothes.

Emma McAuliffe (8)
Balbardie Primary School

THE EXPLOSIVE ERUPTION

It was like I was on the sun,
The eruption was louder than a bass drum,
The magma was as hot as hot water boiled,
The magma was as hot as the sun.

The eruption was like a shaken can of juice,
The magma was flowing down the hill as fast as a flying Ferrari
The lava was as fast as a fast-flowing stream,
The lava was as red as blood.

Ross Harrower (10)
Balbardie Primary School

WINTER

Snow as white as the clouds
Snowflakes like fluttering stars
Icicles dropping like sharp knives
Robin redbreasts jump in the white snow
Winter is very cold!

Sledging like a big shoot
Ice skating, slippery on the ice
Opening presents is fun
Getting cosy in my bed
Can't wait till the next day
Winter is fun and exciting!

Cold fingers and toes
Nearly turned into icicles
Woolly scarves, as warm as your bed
Blue wellies to keep feet warm
Big, woolly socks to keep feet warm
Winter is fun!

Kirstin Ross
Balbardie Primary School

LETHAL LAVA

The volcano erupted like a champagne bottle opening,
It was as hot as the hottest hot chocolate,
It was like loud fireworks exploding,
The lava was as hot as my dad's custard.

The lava was as runny as a yoghurt,
The volcano was like a witch's cauldron bubbling ferociously,
The sticky lava was as sticky as goo,
The volcano was like the sun's blazing heat.

Euan Robertson (11)
Balbardie Primary School

WINTER

The ice is very slidy
The snow is like a sheet of paper
The dark grey clouds are like a boiling kettle
The icicles are like sharp pencils
Winter is super

Christmas is like my birthday
Because you open your presents
Snowballs are great because you get to play
Making snowmen is very cold
Making fairies in the snow is super
Winter is great for me

My woolly jumper is like I have a heater on me
My hat, scarf and gloves keep me warm
When I am playing in the snow
All my woolly clothes make me nice and warm
I wear my hot blanket, watching TV
Winter is very cold for me.

Claire Keenan (8)
Balbardie Primary School

VOLCANO ERUPTION!

At first it erupted like a yoghurt carton bursting,
As fast and furious as an angry cheetah chasing its prey,
As it flows down the side of the volcano,
Like a rocket exploding in mid-air,
Like a balloon bursting,
As hot as a raging fire,
As noisy as a dinosaur roaring at the top of its voice,
Like a witch's cauldron bubbling,
As strong as a furious river.

Aftan Henderson
Balbardie Primary School

WINTER POEM

Winter with hailstones like white cubes falling from the sky
With everything white like a ground painted white
Also with black ice laying on the ground
Including icicles like darts falling down
Winter's white

Sliding across black ice
And having snowball fights with my friends
Making shapes like pyramids in the snow
Sledging down the hill, racing my friends
Winter is brilliant

Wearing big boots
And also a heavy jacket
Feeling very cold
But when having some fun, always very cheerful
Winter is cold.

Brian Crighton
Balbardie Primary School

THE EDINBURGH FEST

The folk all roaring at the band
Playing their song
All of them singing along with the song

The tickets were sold out in 20 minutes
Only two pounds fifty for an adult to enter
The band was getting better every second

They are the best singers
They could rock all morning, night and day.

Ben Young
Balbardie Primary School

WINTER POEM

Gloomy, smoky clouds in the air
Soggy fences, wet and slippy
Snow like a blanket covers everywhere
Icicle like daggers hanging upside down
Winter is great

Snowball fights in the snow
Skiing on ice, slipping and falling down
Catching snowflakes in my mouth
Building snowmen, don't forget its carrot nose
Winter is fun

I'll wear a woolly coat and go out and play
Put on welly boots to keep my feet warm
Put on a scarf to keep my neck warm
I'll put on gloves to throw snowballs
Winter is marvellous.

Dillon Bruce
Balbardie Primary School

LETHAL LAVA

The magma is bubbling like a cauldron
It is as hot as the bright sun beaming down on me
The magma bursts out like a champagne bottle bursting
The volcano is as deadly as a bomb
The lava runs down the side of the volcano like sweat down your face
The lava is bubbling like a baby
It is as hot as the oven
The lava runs down the side of the volcano like a melted
                                        piece of chocolate
The volcano is as deadly as a nuclear bomb
The lava bursts like a yoghurt carton bursting.

Samantha Hogg (10)
Balbardie Primary School

WINTER POEM

Wind whistling like a bird drowning
Gloomy clouds like smoke from a fire
Bare trees like roots spreading out
Puddles like a basin full of water
Winter is great

Drinking hot chocolate topped with marshmallows
Feet in hot water, wriggling my toes
Curling up in my blanket
Playing inside with my toys
Winter is joyful

Woolly jumper made with sheep's wool
Wellies stuffed with wool
Hat with a pompom on top
Gloves knitted by my gran
Winter is my favourite.

Hayley Gibb
Balbardie Primary School

UNTITLED

Running as fast as a cheetah
Flowing like a chocolate river
Bigger than Mount Everest
As big as the world

Burning like a fire
Hotter than an oven
Angry as an ape
As big as the world.

Sarah Hopkinson
Balbardie Primary School

WINTER POEM

A fluffy white blanket everywhere
Dark, grey, gloomy clouds in the sky
Icicles hanging from houses like upside-down ice cream
Smoke coming from a fire, like fog
Winter is great

Sledging around the park
Building snowmen, having fun
Catching snowflakes in my mouth
Having parties all night long
Winter is fun

Woolly clothes, so warm
Hat and gloves - don't forget the scarf!
We all have cold toes
The big socks and boots try to keep me dry
Winter is *super.*

Lucy Moffat (8)
Balbardie Primary School

SOUNDS OF SCHOOL

I hear the sounds of the teacher
Writing on the board
The babbling voices of children
Usually there is the slurping of the milk
I can hear the radiator drip and the clock tick
I can hear something ring
It might be the phone
There is ice falling off the roof
When my friend rolls the dice in a board game.

Steven Gardner (9)
Balbardie Primary School

WINTER POEM

Dark, gloomy clouds,
Icicles like spears,
Snowy-white rooftops,
White fences like very long knives,
Winter is cold.

Opening presents on Christmas Day,
Snowball fights with Ellie,
Building snowmen with Dad,
Going to Christmas parties,
Winter is fun.

Scarves keep your neck warm,
Gloves keep your fingers warm too,
Numb noses and ears,
Cold cheeks and toes,
Winter is chilly.

Alice McCourt
Balbardie Primary School

WINTER POEM

The snow is like a blanket that comes every year
Blue tits jumping all over the ground all day
Animal prints everywhere
Grass poking through the snow
Bare trees are like a man coming along the road
Winter is very, very cold
Making igloos is a lot of fun
Having snowball fights makes you cold
Sledging is easy, how you glide
Winter is full of fun.

James Russell
Balbardie Primary School

WINTER POEM

Ice, a big slide on the ground,
Bare trees like the point of your nail,
Dark clouds like steam from your kettle,
Everywhere white like a bed of wool,
Winter is a *disaster!*

Sledging down the hill,
Snowmen, three balls of snow,
Skating wind pushing you,
Hot chocolate, a whole load of brown snow,
Winter is a whole load of fun.

Scarf, a long warming thing for your neck,
Gloves to warm your fingers,
Cold ears, might fall off,
Cold nose, your nose will freeze,
Winter is cold.

Jennifer Muir (8)
Balbardie Primary School

WINTER POEM

Snow like icing on a Christmas cake
Birds twittering in the cold wind
Icicles like horns on a Viking hat
Snowflakes gently falling to the ground
Winter is peaceful
Igloos like houses, blind with the snow
Snowballs flying through the sky
Cosy in bed, having parties with friends
Ice skating, balancing so you don't fall
Winter is full of happiness.

Kelsey McMorran
Balbardie Primary School

VOLCANO EXPLOSION

A volcano is as fast as a runaway bride,
The lava is as sticky as a lollipop,
A volcano bursts like a water balloon,
Probably slower than the speed of light,
The lava squirts like a water pistol,
The eruption is faster than your ABCs,
It is as hot as a microwave,
The volcano is like a tap running down,
The lava is as bubbly as a bubble bath,
It explodes just like some fireworks,
It is a champagne bottle exploding,
It burns like the sun falling down.

Fiona Hanley
Balbardie Primary School

FEELING DIFFERENT

I feel like nothing,
Nobody to play with me.
I feel frustrated.

I feel excluded.
Nobody knows me today.
I am just useless.

I feel so puzzled.
Nobody likes me today.
I feel quite fed up.

A bowl without soup,
A flower with no petals,
A book without words.

Molly McGiffen (9)
Balbardie Primary School

ERUPTION

When the volcano erupted
It was as fast as Concorde
When the volcano erupted
It was as big as a nuclear bomb
When the volcano erupted
It was like opening a can of shaken juice
When the volcano erupted
It was as tall as the Twin Towers
When the volcano erupted
It was as loud as a nuclear bomb
When the volcano erupted
It was as hot as the sun
When the volcano erupted
It was like a firework exploding
When the volcano erupted
It was as big as the world.

Craig McNeill (10)
Balbardie Primary School

SOUNDS INDOORS AND OUTDOORS

One day I went to the rock night
I heard some music
It was so loud
It was so loud that my eardrums went *pop*
There was the door shutting with a crash
I could hear cars going past
And aeroplanes going *vroom* past the window
It's one in the morning
I can hear the birds tweeting
I can hear my dad snoring and my mum waking up
The clock ticks.

David Baker (9)
Balbardie Primary School

SOUNDS OF SCHOOL

Crash, bash, the sound of books closing
The bubbling of voices next door
The sound of the clock going *tick-tock*
'Shh!' says the teacher
Footsteps walking on the corridor floor
Splash, splash, water dripping from the tap
Swwwish, wipe the pen from the whiteboard
Zzzzzzip goes the zip from a pencil case
Ring, ring goes the phone upstairs
Clitter, clatter go chairs and tables
Suddenly there goes the bell for home time
'Yeah, yeah, yeah!' go the children.

Kimberly Kemp (10)
Balbardie Primary School

CHRISTMAS WITHOUT . . .

Christmas without love would be like the sky without the sun,
It would be like a fire without the flame, a house with no roof,
Christmas without love would be horrible.

Christmas without care would be like a bird with no wings,
It would be like a tree with no roots, a pencil with no lead,
Christmas without care would be terrible.

Christmas without thoughtfulness would be like a boat with no sail,
It would be like a face with no smile, a church with no bell,
Christmas without thoughtfulness would be disgraceful.

Christmas without happiness would be like glitter with no sparkle,
It would be like space with no stars, a book with no words,
Christmas without happiness would be shocking.

Rebekah Bryce Lumsden
Balbardie Primary School

RECIPE FOR A VOLCANO

Take a city as big as London
So happy and cheerful
A happy couple that love each other
And some beautiful horses as white as snow

Add a mountain as big as the Eiffel Tower
Some lava as hot as a kettle that has boiled for a hundred years
And black smoke as misty as fog

Decorate with a moat round the mountain
To catch the bubbling hot lava
A lady that's pregnant
And some babies that have just been born

Stir in a beautiful rabbit just eating away
A wasp's sting
And a boulder to make a splash of lava.

Jordan Lyndon Gibson (11)
Balbardie Primary School

SOUNDS OF SCHOOL

Lots of noise on the stair,
Children running everywhere,
Pencils scraping,
Pupils writing.

Busy working the whole day through,
Keyboards tap-tapping,
Children talking noisily,
The bell ringing for home time.

David Gardiner
Balbardie Primary School

CHRISTMAS WITHOUT . . .

Christmas without love would be a radiator with no heat,
A toilet that doesn't flush, a bird with no wings,
Christmas without love would be a disaster.

Christmas without happiness would be like the sun with no shine,
It would be like a face with no smile, a teddy that's not been stuffed,
Christmas without happiness would be unbearable.

Christmas without caring would be like a baby with no mum,
It would be like winter with no snow, a pen with no ink,
Christmas without caring would be terrible.

Christmas without joy would be like an airport with no planes,
It would be like flowers with no petals, a card with no message,
Christmas without joy would be an outrage.

William Riddell (11)
Balbardie Primary School

CHRISTMAS WITHOUT . . .

Christmas without happiness would be like a world with no love,
It would be like a sea with no waves, a garden without flowers,
Christmas without happiness would be horrible.

Christmas without joy would be like a celebration without family,
It would be like a book with no pages, a house with no walls,
Christmas without joy would be terrible.

Christmas without thought would be like a car with no wheels,
It would be like a ruler that's not straight, a word with no letters,
Christmas without thought would be monstrous.

Christmas without caring would be like turkey with no taste,
It would be like a tap with no water, a face with no smile,
Christmas without caring would be disastrous.

Amber Ferguson (11)
Balbardie Primary School

CHRISTMAS WITHOUT...

Christmas without love would be like a dad with no beer,
It would be like a pencil with no lead, a person with no head,
Christmas without love would be disgraceful.

Christmas without caring would be like a sleigh with no presents,
It would be like a church with no bell,
Christmas without caring would be unbearable.

Christmas without thoughtfulness would be like a candle with no wick,
It would be like a ruler with no cm and a book with no words,
Christmas without thoughtfulness would be upsetting.

Christmas without joy would be like a clock with no hands,
It would be like a CD with no music,
Christmas without joy would be horrible.

Natalie Graham (10)
Balbardie Primary School

CHRISTMAS WITHOUT...

Christmas without joy would be like food with no taste,
A smile with no happiness, a heart with no love,
Christmas without joy would be horrible.

Christmas without love would be like a heart with no beat,
A school with no children, a baby with no mother,
Christmas without love would be unbearable.

Christmas without family would be like a window with no glass,
A face with no smile, a choir with no people,
Christmas without family would be horrid.

Christmas without Santa would be like a book with no words,
A song with no sound, a teacher with no brain,
Christmas without Santa would be dreadful.

Adam Gibb
Balbardie Primary School

CHRISTMAS WITHOUT . . .

Christmas without joy would be like a sea without fish,
It would be like a person with no heart,
A face without eyes,
Christmas without joy would be horrible.

Christmas without thoughtfulness would be like a car with no doors,
It would be like a bird with no feathers,
A box with nothing in it,
Christmas without thoughtfulness would be unhappy.

Christmas without happiness would be like a cat with no tail,
It would be like a tree with no roots,
A clock with no hands,
Christmas without happiness would be heartbreaking.

Christmas without love would be like a pencil with no lead,
It would be like a flower with no petals,
A table with no legs,
Christmas without love would be like nothing on Earth.

Fiona Stephen (10)
Balbardie Primary School

VOLCANOES ERUPTING

The lava was hot as a microwave,
The lava was so hot I felt like I was in an oven,
It's like bursting, bubbling bubbles,
It was really hot for my mum
And she was bursting red.

The lava was as hot as curry,
It's like it was a piece of stone,
It's hot as the sun,
As hot as the radiator.

Kristina Wainwright
Balbardie Primary School

RECIPE FOR A VOLCANO

Take a friendly, attractive village in the Highlands,
Intelligent animals and a river that runs through the village,
As smooth as sand.

Add a hill as high as the sky,
Some magma and lava waiting to erupt
And smoke shooting out as swift as a train.

Decorate with smoke, as black as night,
Lava as scorching as the bright sun
And lava waiting to burst.

Stir in the madness of the people running for their lives,
The sadness of the child's tears and the anxiety of the animals.

Nicole Little
Balbardie Primary School

THE ZOO

I can hear the crocodile snapping,
I can hear the lions roaring,
I can hear the seals clapping,
I can hear the giraffes breaking twigs.

I can hear the elephants trumpeting,
I can hear the fish plopping,
I can hear the birds cheeping,
I can hear the rattle of the snakes.

I can hear the frogs ribbiting,
I can hear the bees buzzing,
I can hear the bats flapping,
I can hear the splashing of polar bears.

Frank McMichael (9)
Balbardie Primary School

CHRISTMAS WITHOUT . . .

Christmas without care would be like a jotter without pages,
It would be like a fist with no bone, a piece of chocolate
with no texture,
Christmas without care would be scary.

Christmas without love would be like a plane with no wings,
It would be like a bird with no feathers, a car with no wheels,
Christmas without love would be horrific.

Christmas without joy would be like a star with no light,
It would be like a piece of snow with no coldness, a house
with no walls,
Christmas without joy would be rubbish.

Christmas without happiness would be like a cake with no sponge,
It would be like a car with no engine, a bus with no people,
Christmas without happiness would be unhappy.

Steven Hill
Balbardie Primary School

AS HOT AS CURRY

The volcano bubbles like my fish at home,
The lava is as sticky as goo,
The lava is as hot as curry
And as hot as Dad's custard,
It is as bright as a light in my eye.

It's really hot, it's like your mum's oven,
It is as hot as fire,
It's really noisy like fireworks,
It's like popping popcorn,
It's shooting up in the air like a bottle bursting.

Jade Fullerton
Balbardie Primary School

CHRISTMAS WITHOUT...

Christmas without love would be like a river without water,
It would be like Santa without a sack, a paper with no letters,
Christmas without love would be disastrous.

Christmas without happiness would be like a clock without numbers,
It would be like a table without legs, a tree without leaves,
Christmas without happiness would be unbearable.

Christmas without joy would be like a face without a smile,
It would be like a garden without flowers, a rainbow without colours,
Christmas without joy would be horrible.

Christmas without thoughtfulness would be like children without toys,
It would be like a baby without a mother, a boy without presents,
Christmas without thoughtfulness would be unforgivable.

Lauren Kelly (10)
Balbardie Primary School

FEELING DIFFERENT

Left out, I feel mad.
I have no friends, feeling bad.
I am so upset.

Play time is over.
I am a book without words.
What have I done wrong?

I am worth nothing.
Everybody dislikes me.
No one talks to me.

I am unwanted.
I am the clock with no hands.
I feel so depressed.

Emily Spalding
Balbardie Primary School

CHRISTMAS WITHOUT . . .

Christmas without happiness would be like a concert
                                    without the people,
It would be like a mouth with no teeth, a head with no brains,
Christmas without happiness would be terrible.

Christmas without joy would be like a boat with no sails,
It would be like a rainbow with no colours, a book with no words,
Christmas without joy would be horrible.

Christmas without love would be like a film with no pictures,
It would be like a football game with no players, a body with no heart,
Christmas without love would be a disaster.

Christmas without thoughtfulness would be like an airport
                                    with no planes,
It would be like a door with no handle, a church with no bells,
Christmas without thoughtfulness would be unbearable.

Lewis Proudfoot
Balbardie Primary School

FEELING DIFFERENT

In the back playground,
I feel frustrated and sad,
Like a nobody.

I feel down, so down.
Why do they hate me so much?
Why don't they like me?

In the school classroom,
I feel like nothing at all.
Why are they like this?

Craig Brown-Campbell
Balbardie Primary School

CHRISTMAS WITHOUT . . .

Christmas without joy would be like a cake with no candles,
It would be like Father Christmas with no sack, a chocolate
with no taste,
Christmas without joy would be a disaster.

Christmas without love would be like a Santa with no beard,
It would be like a train with no wheels, a boy with no ball,
Christmas without love would be horrible.

Christmas without happiness would be like a clock with no face,
It would be like a bird with no feathers, a farm with no animals,
Christmas without happiness would be monstrous.

Christmas without thoughtfulness would be like a fire with no flame,
It would be like a room with no people, a box with no chocolates,
Christmas without thoughtfulness would be horrid.

Joshua Fleming
Balbardie Primary Schoo

FEELING DIFFERENT

Alone with no friends,
I have no one to play with.
Feeling so lonely.

I feel like nothing,
I am so sad and lonely.
I'm the ship that sank.

I'm the left-out child,
I have this sinking feeling,
That I am no one.

Claire Inglis (9)
Balbardie Primary School

RECIPE FOR A VOLCANO

Grab five happy little children playing in the stream,
A glistening, sparkling, peaceful waterfall
And some golden eagles from their nest.

Add one screaming baby, two growling dogs
And one spooky, crooked, black mountain.

Pour in bubbling lava, some spurting magma
Waiting to burst out of the hole at the top
And some hot, burning rock.

Stir in the sound of the terrified people,
The galloping hooves of the horses
And the praying silence of the minister,
Stir it all up and
Run for your lives!

Rachel Arkless (10)
Balbardie Primary School

FEELING DIFFERENT

I felt uncared for.
I was lonely at the time.
I was really sad.

I was so angry.
I am a frog with no leap.
No one would help me.

I was feeling mad.
I really wish I had friends.
I'm always left out.

Jade Lamb
Balbardie Primary School

CHRISTMAS WITHOUT . . .

Christmas without love would be like space with no sun,
It would be like a word with no meaning, a house with no foundation,
Christmas without love would be terrible.

Christmas without happiness would be like a present with nothing in it,
It would be like a world with no people, a cake with no candles,
Christmas without happiness would be shocking.

Christmas without joy would be like a keyboard with no keys,
It would be like a star with no light, a family without friends,
Christmas without joy would be rubbish.

Christmas without thoughtfulness would be like a flute with no music,
It would be like a knife with no blade, a bin with no litter,
Christmas without thoughtfulness would be junk.

Lauchlan Brown (10)
Balbardie Primary School

CHRISTMAS WITHOUT . . .

Christmas without caring would be like politics with no vile attitude,
It would be like love with no passion, a twist with no turn,
Christmas without caring would be regretful.

Christmas without love would be like Romeo without Juliet,
It would be like a book with no story, chocolate with no cocoa beans,
Christmas without love would be worthless.

Christmas without joy would be like summer with no sun,
It would be like a season with no weather, like war with no victory,
Christmas without joy would be painful.

Christmas without happiness would be like a fire with no flame,
It would be like a horse with no hoof, a camel with no hump,
Christmas without happiness would be ruined.

Murray McLean (9)
Balbardie Primary School

WINTER

Robin redbreast hopping around
Snowflakes flutter like stars twinkling in the air
Dark, grey clouds covering the sun
Snow as white as feathers fluttering in the air
Winter is cold and a fun time

Getting cosy in bed, can't wait until the next day
Ice skating all day long, what fun it is to play
Sledging up and down the *big, big* hill
Making delicious food to feast upon
Winter is really exciting

Woolly hat and gloves to keep you warm
Fluffy earmuffs for your red, nippy ears
Cold fingers and toes with the cold and windy days
A cosy jumper to keep your body warm
Winter is cold and frosty.

Emma Wilson
Balbardie Primary School

FEELING DIFFERENT

I am so lonely,
Out here all on my own now.
I wish I had friends.

I feel unwanted.
I'm all on my own now.
I feel very sad.

A book without words,
I am so very upset.
I feel very scared.

Steven Gray (10)
Balbardie Primary School

WINTER

Snow fluttering to the ground
Like God dropping wool from the sky.
Bare trees covered with snow
Like a white blanket on the tree.
Blizzard blowing snow off roofs
Like someone on top.
Icicles hanging from doorways
Like knives trying to chop you up.
Winter is fun.
Everyone having snowball fights,
Snowboarding like falling off a skyscraper.
Sledging down steep hills,
Putting up Christmas trees
Like planting in the garden.
Winter is cold.

Lee McIlroy (8)
Balbardie Primary School

FEELING DIFFERENT

Today I am sad.
I feel like no one loves me.
I feel I'm hated.

I'm in the playground,
I feel so down in the dumps.
I'm extremely sad.

I am a sad boy.
I'm a bone with no marrow.
I'm so hopeless.

Nathan McGrorty (10)
Balbardie Primary School

WINTER

Ice like a huge lake in a fridge
Snow all over my house
Icicles all over the trees
Bare trees covered in snow
Winter is very, very cold

Sledging is good, good fun
Building igloos is good for shelter
Putting up the Christmas tree is a good help
Skiing is very good
Winter is really good fun

A woolly scarf is very cosy
Fluffy earmuffs are good for the ears
Blue wellies are good in the snow
Big, woolly socks are very warm
Winter is very, very, very cold.

Connor Rae (8)
Balbardie Primary School

FEELING DIFFERENT

Flower without leaves,
A sharpener with no blade,
I am so depressed.

Nothing that's special.
Soon I'll be really mad.
I am so depressed.

I am so annoyed.
No one likes me for I'm mad.
I am so depressed.

Maxwell Yates
Balbardie Primary School

WINTER

Snowflakes fluttering from the dark clouds
Robin redbreasts flying in the air
Fluttering snowflakes dropping on the roof
Icicles hanging from the shed
Winter is fun

Snowmen everywhere
Snowballs flying all over the place
Sledging down deep hills
Snow angels on the ground
Winter is fun

Cosy jumpers keep you warm
Green wellies keep you dry
Big, woolly socks keep you warm
Woolly gloves keep you warm
Winter is fun.

Declan McMillan (9)
Balbardie Primary School

VOLCANO EXPLOSION

A volcano is as hot as a bursting fire,
It bursts open like a balloon bursting,
The lava is as red as red wine,
It is as noisy as a dinosaur growling,
The lava is as bubbly as bubbles in a bath,
When it explodes it is like a firework exploding,
Stones and rocks coming out of the volcano
Sound like elephants' feet hitting the ground,
When the volcano is finished,
It is as silent as a mouse.

Nicole Osborne
Balbardie Primary School

WINTER

Snow dropping off houses
Robin redbreasts jumping fence to fence
Snowflakes falling down on heads
Animal prints of Rudolph and the reindeer taking off
Winter is cold and dark at night

Snowboarding in the morning in the snow
Having snowball fights with my friends
Making snowmen with my friends
Getting cosy in bed for the night
Winter is full of adventures

Cold fingers and ears from running around in the snow
Woolly hat and gloves to keep me warm
Big, woolly socks so snow doesn't get in
A cosy jumper to stay warm
Winter is fun.

Lauren Gillogley (9)
Balbardie Primary School

VOLCANO

Like a yoghurt carton bursting,
As hot as my mum's cooker,
As fast as a lion,
As fast as a jet,
It's like a carton of milk flying in the sky
It's like boys fitting in a pie
As fast as darkness and is sticky as goo
Watch out, you could be as hot as the sun.

Lee Brown
Balbardie Primary School

WINTER POEM

Icicles are sharp horns of a Viking hat
Snow is like a blanket covering everywhere
A howling wind could blow tiles off the roof
Snowflakes are a fluttering star falling to the ground
Winter is a fun season but very cold

Snowboarding is really fun, I could do it forever
Ice skating's good for keeping really healthy
Skiing is really skilful for pulling good tricks
Sledging is good for a lovely breeze
Winter is good for a nice bit of fun

My woolly socks have my feet warm in a second
A woolly hat and gloves keep you really warm
A cosy scarf will have your neck nice and warm
A warm jumper for a nice cosy person
Winter is a lovely time but freezing cold.

James Dunsmore (8)
Balbardie Primary School

FEELING DIFFERENT

I'm always lonely,
I'm a mouse without a tail.
I wish I had friends.

They were whispering,
Most probably about me.
They always do that.

It's play time right now,
I do not want to go out.
Why don't they like me?

Claire Marshall (9)
Balbardie Primary School

WINTER POEM

Animal prints like prints on a biscuit
Snow like icing on a cake
Icicles like sharp horns
Robin redbreasts landing in my garden
Winter is cold, fun and snowy

Ice skating is fun and good and I go down the hill
Opening Christmas presents is fun
Decorating Christmas trees is fun, good and great
Snow angels is fun, good and great
Winter is cold, nice and fun

Tingly fingers and toes
Cosy, fluffy jackets to keep you warm
Thick gloves and scarves make you hot
Fluffy earmuffs keep you warm
Winter is chilly but fun.

Stacy McAllen (9)
Balbardie Primary School

FEELING DIFFERENT

Never any good,
I am very frustrated.
I am unwanted.

I am sad and mad.
I am nothing important.
In the front playground.

I feel frustrated.
I am a snake with no fangs.
I feel really sad.

Christopher Kellas (9)
Balbardie Primary School

Winter Poem

Icicles like the horn of a rhino
Animal prints scattered on the ground
Snow like icing on a cake
Robins jumping around the trees
Winter is fun and chilly

Having snowball fights
Putting up the Christmas tree
Opening Christmas presents
Getting cosy in bed
Winter is fun

Cold toes and cold fingers
Woolly hat and gloves
A warm, woolly scarf
A cosy jumper
Winter is cold and white.

Brogan Donaldson (9)
Balbardie Primary School

WINTER POEM

Snow is like icing on a cake
Icicles hanging from a rooftop like sharp knives
Dark grey clouds like cotton wool
Snowflakes fluttering from the sky
Winter is fun for everyone

Going snowboarding on high hills
Making snowmen is really, really good fun!
Going sledging is exciting
Having snowball fights with my friends,
Winter is amazing!

Big, wellie boots to keep my feet dry
Woolly hat and gloves to keep my head and hands cosy
A big, warm, cosy jumper so I am nice and warm
Big, woolly socks for my feet to keep warm
Winter is fantastic.

Christopher Murton (9)
Balbardie Primary School

WINTER

Snow like a big white blanket
Icicles like big, sharp knives
Snowflakes fluttering to the ground
Gales blowing the branches on the trees
Winter is snowy

Making snowmen in the snow
Snowboarding at the park
Skiing at the competition
Sledging near your house
Winter is fun

Big, woolly socks to keep my feet warm
Fluffy earmuffs go around my ears
A warm, woolly scarf goes around my neck
A cosy jumper keeps my body cosy.

Daniel Sysa
Balbardie Primary School

WINTER

Snow like icing sprinkling on a cake
Storm, breaking wind going by the window
Breezy, the sound of a flash passing by
Icicles, the tip shivering
Winter is a memory of joy with all the breeze

Adventuring in the snowflakes
Sledging, trying to bear the wind
Ice skating, the marks on the ice
Making igloos, the home of winter
Winter is exciting and full of joy

Woolly earmuffs that slide on my ears
Blue wellies that let me splash in the slush
My woolly socks that keep my feet cosy
A cold feeling that runs up my spine
Winter is a feeling of family.

Emily Binnie
Balbardie Primary School

WINTER

Snow like a white blanket covering the ground
Robin redbreasts jumping about merrily
Bare trees like lots of pencils joined together
Icicles like daggers hanging from the roof
Winter is snowy and fun

Sledging down steep hills
Ice skating round the ice rink
Making igloos and sitting in them
Opening Christmas presents to see what I get
Winter is full of joy

Green wellies to stop snow getting to my feet
A woolly hat to keep my ears warm
Cold toes and fingers if I stay out too long
A cold face if I don't wear my balaclava.

Ross Allan
Balbardie Primary School

WINTER

Snowflakes flutter down
Like hailstones in a storm
Robin redbreasts cuddle up in their warm nests to hibernate
Animal prints fade away when more snow falls
Winter is fun because I get to ice skate

Sledging is full of joy and laughter
I love winter because I love sliding on the ice
Skiing is something you need to be careful at
Winter is cold but very nice

My woolly hat, scarf and glove set is purple
And too warm to take off
Wellies keep my feet warm and dry
A cosy jumper is for keeping me warm
Winter is when there are clouds in the sky.

Jennifer Marshall
Balbardie Primary School

WINTER POEM

Snow is like cotton wool
Robin redbreasts flying in the air
Icicles hanging from rooftops looking like daggers
Snowflakes fluttering onto the fresh snow
Winter is fun with snowflakes fluttering around

Sledging is great, going fast in the snow
Making snowmen is fun, tying a long scarf around his neck
In the evening it is nice getting cosy in bed
On Christmas Day it is fun opening all your presents
Winter is fun when you make lovely snow angels

When you're out, you should put on your woolly hat, scarf and gloves
To keep you nice and warm
Cosy jumpers, nice and warm just ready to go out and play
A nice pair of socks to keep my feet warm
In winter you need a nice warm jacket
Winter is all about wearing a hat, scarf and gloves.

Erin Moffat (8)
Balbardie Primary School

WINTER

Robin redbreasts sitting on the bench
Snow on the grass
Storm blowing other trees
Ice on the lake

Winter is stormy and snowy

Making snowmen is fun
Playing in the snow makes me laugh
Skiing down a hill
Snowboarding at the park

Winter is really fun

Blue wellies to keep me dry
Fluffy earmuffs to keep my ears hot
Big, woolly socks to keep my feet really warm
A warm, woolly scarf to keep my neck warm

Winter is cold.

James Hampson (8)
Balbardie Primary School

WINTER

Robin redbreasts chirping in the trees
Icicles hanging from the roof
Like a bull's horn
Animals' footprints in the snow
Snow on the ground like a mass of rubber flakes
Winter is fun

Making snowmen is fun
Having a snowball fight
Gets me covered in snow
I always want to get into my cosy bed
Adventuring in the snow
Always gets me lost
Winter is cold

My woolly hat to keep my ears warm
A woolly scarf wrapped round my neck
A woolly jumper to keep me warm
Big woolly socks up to my knees
Winter is cold so I wear warm clothes.

Ellie McCourt
Balbardie Primary School

WINTER

The snow is a white blanket
Can you believe the trees so bare?
No leaves, I am shocked
Ice is hard and can hurt people

Winter is shocking

Sledging down the hills
Making snowmen
Opening presents on Christmas Day
Making fairies

Winter is fun

Woolly jumper, nice and warm
Drinking hot chocolate
Having fun putting my scarf on
My slippers keeping my toes warm

Winter is *great*.

Noor Zulfiguar
Balbardie Primary School

WHAT IS THE SUN?

It's a ball of burning fire
that rests in the second sky.
It's aged beyond age,
though to our innocent eyes it's young,
our beautiful, beautiful sun.

It must be lonely up there,
floating around in space.
Its one and only interest,
to stay hidden from the moon,
our beautiful, beautiful sun.

It sits up there watching,
watches us having fun,
while we're playing with our friends.
It can only watch,
our beautiful, beautiful sun.

That's not all it has to watch,
it has to watch our pain,
it wishes it could comfort us
or even feel the same,
our beautiful, beautiful sun.

Yet we don't care for it,
though it gives us life itself.
So I hope you feel sorry for
our beautiful, beautiful sun.

Katie Cunningham
Balbardie Primary School

WHAT IS THE SUN?

The sun is like a fiery sphere,
Burning all of the horrible, cold snow on a winter night,
It is like an orange tangerine,
Lying in a huge fruit bowl.

The sun is like a blazing bowl,
Looking over us in the early morning.
It is like a boiling, golden frisbee,
Soaring across the huge mountains.

The sun is like a bright yellow torch,
Flying across the Highlands.
A giant burning fireball,
Dropping when the sun sets in the night.

The sun is a circular, red apple,
Watching over us when we are in town.
It is like God in Heaven,
Staring down at us from above.

We all love the sun,
Because without it,
We would never be alive.

David Ferguson
Balbardie Primary School

WHAT IS THE SUN?

The sun is a bright spark,
whizzing out of a fire.
It is an orange berry
hanging on top of the biggest tree.

The sun is a golden chickenpox
dancing on your face.
It is a yellow Mr Man
bobbing down a street of stars.

The sun is a pair of yellow polka dot shorts
stretching on your dad's legs.
It is a yellow, smiley face
rolling outer space.

The sun is a bright orange frisbee
zooming into a dog's mouth.
It is an orange-yellow sunflower
swaying in the background.

You should be thankful the sun is just a sun
and nothing else.

Amy Scotson
Balbardie Primary School

WHAT IS THE SUN?

The sun is as round as a ball,
all blown up for a football match.
It's round like Santa's belly,
after eating all the biscuits!

The sun is yellow like a banana
that's not just ripe yet.
It's round and golden,
like a brand new pound coin.

The sun is up high in the sky,
above the clouds and everything else.
It stays up in the sky,
switched on all day to give us light.

The sun is like a buttercup
that's swaying in the wind.
At the start, I didn't know what the sun was,
but now I do!

Steffani Beaton
Balbardie Primary School

WHAT IS THE SUN?

The sun is like a big yellow ball
whizzing about in the air
It is as hot as a fire
burning in a cold living room

The sun is a flying saucer
zooming through the air
It is as golden as a sunflower
waving in the sky

The sun is like a yellow iced doughnut
sitting on a cloud
It is like a golden apple
flying towards the moon

The sky is a street light
shining down to Earth
It is a hot beam of a shining torch
peering over the mountains

The sun can be anything.

Mandy Strachan
Balbardie Primary School

WHAT IS THE SUN?

The sun is like a buttercup
swaying in the wind
It is like a Smartie
in the Smartie tub

The sun is like a fire
burning in the living room
It is like a group of stars
shining so very brightly

The sun is like a football
kicked right high in the sky
It is like a light bulb
waiting to be switched on

The sun is round as a ball
ready for a netball match
It is like a big cookie
just come from a cooker

That is what I think of the sun
But the sun is just the sun.

Clare Richardson
Balbardie Primary School

THEME PARK SOUNDS

I can hear a firework display,
I can hear a crashing boat,
I can hear guns going off at the shooting game,
I can hear motorbikes on the motorway,
I can see people shouting at each other,
I can see a plane getting ready to fly,
In the café, computers getting set up for the day,
I can hear the bell of people winning the hardest games,
I can see a person being sick on a ride,
I can hear a ride making a big noise,
I can hear a little baby crying in his mum's arms,
I can see a person shooting the target with a gun,
I can see a few people going into the haunted house,
Then I had to go home
But there will be another time at the theme park.

Alistair Gauld (10)
Balbardie Primary School

HARBOUR SOUNDS

I wake up and hear the rumble of the cars
And the scratch of thorns on the window.
I hear the fizz in the workshop and the grinding of drills.
I hear whirling of propellers and *chuffa chuffa* of engines.
I hear dripping of the rain from the gutter.
I hear the rustling of bags from the shop.
I hear the bell of the shop tinkling and voices of well-known people.
Clinking chains being dragged across the dirt road.
I hear the squelching of mud and *splat* someone falling
And shouting, 'Got you conk!'
I hear my dad saying, 'Are you going to like it here?'
Then I reply, 'Yes, I will!'

Sophie Stewart (10)
Balbardie Primary School

SOUNDS OF THE ZOO

The sound of people's cars coming into the zoo,
The sound of people parking their cars and turning the engine off
And then closing the door,
The sound of people's shoes scraping along the ground,
The sound of monkeys chattering while people walk by them,
I can hear the flap of the waddling penguins' flippers while they walk,
I can hear the little children screaming while they walk past the
                                        lions and the tigers,
I can hear lots of people laughing at the funny animals climbing
                                and clambering onto the cage,
I can hear the snakes saying *ssssss* and them slithering
                                along the ground,
The sound of the kids running away from the giraffes,
I can hear the till closing as somebody buys something from the shop,
I can hear the lady or man's voice, 'The zoo is closing in 10 minutes!'
Then I can hear everybody getting into the car and going home.

Kirsten Sharkey
Balbardie Primary School

SOUNDS OF SCHOOL

The excited chatter of children.
The chime of the bell.
The boots scraping, going up the stairs.
The door creaking as I open it.
The computer starting up.
The chairs scraping on the floor.
The teacher's voice.
The paper going whizz.
The squeak of the chalk.
The *sssh* of the teacher.
The jotters getting handed out.
The roar of the blackboard.
Our pencils going mad.
Our pencil cases going zip.

Gemma Linkston (9)
Balbardie Primary School

FEELING DIFFERENT

Nothing important!
A flower with no petals,
Never any good.

Nobody likes me.
Dejected, lonely, anxious,
Frustrated and sad.

Freckles and glasses,
Crooked teeth and curly hair.
I feel so upset.

Alexis Saunders (9)
Balbardie Primary School

SIMPLE SOUNDS OF SCHOOL

The chattering of my friends,
The clanging of the bell,
The scraping of boots,
The stomping of shoes going upstairs.

Our teacher's loud, booming voice,
Our pencil cases going zip,
Our jotters being handed out,
Our class settling down.

The roaring of the blackboard,
The squeak of the chalk,
The giggle of my friends,
The *sssh* of the teacher.

Our pencils scribbling away,
Our paper ripping constantly,
Our chairs scraping on the floor,
Our teacher saying, 'Be quiet!'

The rumble of my tummy,
The ring of the bell,
The excitement of the children,
The pitter-patter of shoes.

Our mouths munching away,
Our bodies full of energy,
Our hearts pumping quickly,
Our legs getting tired

And we start chatting again.

Rosie Sterrick (9)
Balbardie Primary School

SOUNDS OF SCHOOL

One morning at school, a pencil fell onto the floor
And the door made a creaky noise.
The chalk was noisy on the blackboard
And then next door were noisy and you could hear voices from them.
Then the tables started to move
And the teacher started shouting.
She dropped a bit of paper onto the floor
And you could hear the clock ticking
And my book dropped off my desk and the bell went for play time.
When we went outside, all the children were so noisy
And they were running around crazy,
The sound of the bell is *ding!*
When we were outside we heard a crash
And the teachers came out and got the lines.
The teacher started to talk and we got on with our work
And now all of our class is nice and calm.
It was seven minutes to home time, we got our classroom tidy,
Then we got a story, it was about sounds,
It was nearly home time and we got ready
And the bell went and we went out of school.

Natasha McLeod
Balbardie Primary School

FEELING DIFFERENT

In the school playground,
I am feeling so fed up.
I wish I had friends.

I am feeling sad.
Oh why? Oh why? Oh why me?
I feel very scared.

I feel uncared for.
I hate my ugly freckles.
I feel really mad.

I feel so silly.
I am a snake with no fangs.
I am unwanted.

Leona Smith (9)
Balbardie Primary School

ERUPTION

Volcano erupting as loud as a nuclear bomb strike
The lava was as hot as if the sun had exploded
The lava got to be as fast as a fully-tuned Ferrari
Ash was as bright as the sun

The lava was as red as blood
The eruption was like a champagne bottle opening
The volcano was as rocky as the moon
The lava flowed as long as the Great Wall of China.

Jonathan Menzies (10)
Balbardie Primary School

WHAT IS THE SUN?

The sun is a huge ball of gas
Soaring in the sky.
It is a golden bubble
Gleaming way up high.

The sun is like a juicy melon
Peeping from the trees.
It is a primrose circle
Flying past the leaves.

The sun is a red-hot planet
Hovering high above.
It is a sparkling tangerine
Gliding like a dove.

The sun is like a scarlet ruby
Shimmering over the sea.
It is a burning golden ball
Shining just for me.

Louise Rankine
Balbardie Primary School

WHAT IS THE SUN?

The sun is an orange bubble
Rising past my window.
It is a blinding light
Shooting up to the sky.

The sun is a ball of fire
Burning like a giant star.
It is a massive sphere of gas
Bouncing over space.

The sun is a bright crimson bird
Flitting through the air.
It is a cut tangerine
Seeping into the clouds.

The sun is a scarlet god
Falling over the horizon.
It is the light of the world
Setting in the distance.

Brionna Wilson
Balbardie Primary School

WHAT IS THE SUN?

The sun is an amber ball
Thrown up to the sky.
The sun is a yellow light
Shining on you and I.

The sun is a cheery face
Looking down on the world.
It is a great big heater
Chasing off the cold.

The sun is a bright flower,
The biggest of them all.
It is a fantastic sight
When it's about to fall.

The sun is a round person
That dwells up in the sky.
It is a shining star
Shooting through the sky.

Lauren Barclay
Balbardie Primary School

What Is The Sun?

The sun is a giant yellow ball
Hovering in the air.
It is a primrose scorching circle
Drifting in the sky.

The sun is a burning ball of fire
Shooting through the air.
It is travelling at amazing speed
Floating into space.

The sun is like a flying saucer
Reflecting on the Earth.
It is burning hot, so watch out,
Beautiful it may be.

The sun is a giant sphere of gas
Shining like the moon.
It is a golden liquid
Devolving in the clouds.

Samantha Kerr
Balbardie Primary School

WHAT IS THE SUN?

The sun is an amber balloon
Rising over the horizon.
It is a huge ball of gas
Hiding in the clouds.

The sun is a scarlet ball
Reflecting in the water.
It is a golden bubble
Floating through the air.

The sun is a golden bird
Soaring through outer space.
It is a boiling pot
Flitting behind the hill.

The sun is a primrose disk
Setting beneath the town.
It is an orange sphere
Falling from our sight.

Robyn Young
Balbardie Primary School

WHAT IS THE SUN?

The sun is a ball of gas
Setting in the sky.
It is a golden balloon
Floating round and round.

The sun is a great ball of fire
Drifting up and down.
It is as round as a football
Reflecting in the water.

The sun is yellow and orange,
Which sets over the hill.
It is as bright as a bulb
Rising all the way round.

The sun is a golden sunflower
High up in the sky.
It is like the Earth's light bulb
Which never burns out.

Chris Mclean
Balbardie Primary School

WHAT IS THE SUN?

The sun is like a red-hot bubble
Floating round the sky.
It is a golden tangerine
Thrown into the air.

The sun is a yellow ball
Bounced into the air.
It is a giant penny
Flicked into space.

The sun is outside my window,
Waiting to set.
It is a golden Smartie
Hiding behind the trees.

The sun is over there,
It's glowing in colour.
It is a painted portrait
Splashed into outer space.

Clare Farrell
Balbardie Primary School

FEELING DIFFERENT

I am so lonely.
I am really unhappy.
I wish I had friends.

I feel really sad.
I am a snake with no fangs.
I am unwanted.

I am really scared.
I am feeling excluded.
I feel really mad.

I am uncared for.
I am a tree with no leaves.
I am so fed up.

I am nobody.
I am never any good.
I am so annoyed.

Alexander MacLeod (10)
Balbardie Primary School

FEELING DIFFERENT

Outside, before school,
I stand lonely and depressed.
I feel unwanted.

I feel miserable.
I am the bee with no sting.
I wish I had friends.

I am excluded.
I am a frog with no jump.
I'm a nobody!

I'm the different one,
With no friends whatsoever.
I am so upset.

I heard them talking,
Whispering about me, course
They always do that.

I am really, really sad.
I'm the book with no pages
That nobody reads.

Ashleigh Nelson
Balbardie Primary School

FEELING DIFFERENT

Nobody likes me.
I am sad and unwanted.
Why do they hate me?

What have I done wrong
That makes them treat me like this?
Am I just hopeless?

I've freckles and spots,
My glasses are big and red,
Is that the reason?

Am I the class dunce?
Am I the book with no name?
The dog with no bitc?

Oh why, oh why me?
The girl waiting for a chance.
I'm no use at all.

Ayley Wilson (9)
Balbardie Primary School

FEELING DIFFERENT

In the living room,
I was feeling very sad.
I cheered myself up.

In the school playground,
I was angry and upset.
I made things better.

But soon after that,
The bullies came and called names
To everybody.

Tomorrow they are in for a shock,
The head teacher
Will go to see them.

No more bullying!
It's at an end forever.
They know better now.

Dylan Ross
Balbardie Primary School

FEELING DIFFERENT

In the front playground,
I feel ignored and left out.
I feel unwanted.

I feel uncared for.
I have no friends to play with.
I'm very upset.

When I have my lunch,
When I have my play time,
They're out to get me.

I feel so depressed.
It is really upsetting.
They really hurt me.

It is so unfair!
I can hear them whispering.
I am so depressed.

Debbie Young
Balbardie Primary School

FEELING DIFFERENT

I am just useless!
I have no one to play with.
I'm like a nothing.

I don't have a friend.
Certainly unwanted here,
By everyone else.

Nobody knows me.
I'm a book without a name,
Left out, unlike you.

I'm an ugly child,
I now believe that it's true.
I'm paint, wet, untouched.

The bully hurts me.
I am the clock without hands.
I'm getting nowhere.

Peter Ferguson (10)
Balbardie Primary School

WHAT IS THE SUN?

The sun is an orange wheel,
Dangling from the clouds.
It is a lemon sunflower,
Burning brightly in the hills.

The sun is an amber football,
Glowing gorgeously above your head.
It is a crimson circle,
Floating happily in the sky.

The sun is a ruby pancake,
Flying gracefully from above.
It is a golden doughnut,
Sailing smoothly above the houses.

The sun is an orange sphere,
Shining cheerfully amid the clouds.
It is a scarlet daisy
Scorching rapidly in space.

Alastair Binnie (11)
Balbardie Primary School

WHAT IS THE SUN?

The sun is a golden wheel,
Drifting calmly in the sky.
It is a crimson hula-hoop,
Scorching happily in space.

The sun is an amber coin,
Sailing slowly down the hill.
It is an orange balloon,
Burning brightly in the sky.

The sun is a scarlet button,
Floating feather-like past the waterfall.
It is a yellow dandelion,
Twinkling brightly above the river.

The sun is a terracotta sphere,
Bouncing casually in the clouds.
It is a bubble,
Gliding in the air.

Kimberley Jarvis (11)
Balbardie Primary School

WHAT IS THE SUN?

The sun is an orange,
Floating in the sky.
It is a bouncy ball,
Bouncing in an out of the sky.

The sun is a yellow sphere,
With a burning, jagged edge.
It is an orange button
On a cardigan.

The sun is a red ball,
Tumbling in the air.
It is a burning balloon,
Rolling around the universe.

The sun is an amber Ferris wheel,
Spinning round at the fair.
It is a dandelion with water on the top,
Glistening brightly.

Gary Scott (11)
Balbardie Primary School

WHAT IS THE SUN?

The sun is a red, bouncy ball,
Bouncing casually in the sky.
It is a yellow hula-hoop,
Flying through space.

The sun is a golden coin,
Drifting through the clouds.
It is a lemon Polo,
Sailing through the universe.

The sun is an omelette,
Scorching happily in the air.
It is a cheese pizza,
Shining cheerfully above the river.

The sun is a bubble,
Hovering above us.
It is a scarlet button,
Burning brightly throughout the world.

Kristopher Kaul (11)
Balbardie Primary School

WHAT IS THE SUN?

The sun is an amber Jaffa Cake,
With a soft jelly centre.
It is a ruby Smartie,
Shining cheerfully in the sky.

The sun is a golden ball,
Bouncing in the sky.
It is a rose wheel,
Running rapidly through space.

The sun is a giant egg yolk,
Dripping through the air.
It is a scarlet balloon,
Floating above us.

The sun is a red tomato,
Rolling softly in the clouds.
It is a golden CD,
Scorching brightly in the sky.

Aimee Cameron (11)
Balbardie Primary School

WHAT IS THE SUN?

The sun is an orange clock,
Floating gently across the world.
It is a crimson wheel,
Sleeping soundly at night.

The sun is a golden ball,
Scorching rapidly on humans.
It is a scarlet CD,
Gliding casually all around.

The sun is a lovely round doughnut,
Melting us slowly and quietly.
It is a lemon hula-hoop,
Simply shining upon us.

The sun is a red ruby,
Glistening wonderfully in the clouds.
It is a rose button,
Burning brightly on the world.

Rachel MacLeod (11)
Balbardie Primary School

What Is The Sun?

The sun is a red ball,
Bouncing in the sky.
It's a tangerine,
Skimming through the air.

The sun is a golden wheel,
Spinning in the sky.
It is a pancake,
Spinning rapidly in the sky.

The sun is a yellow button,
Floating in the sky.
It is a baseball,
Being tossed into space.

The sun is a scarlet Revel,
Sailing softly in the air.
It is a Minstrel,
Burning brightly in the sky.

Gordon Mackinnon (10)
Balbardie Primary School

FEELING DIFFERENT

Alone with no friends,
I feel lonely and frightened,
Treated like some soil.

I feel like nothing,
Frustrated and excluded,
Left out and fed up.

Furious and sad,
Unpopular and annoyed,
Never any good.

Unloved and hated,
I am a bird without wings,
I'm not liked at all.

Glen Ross
Balbardie Primary School

OUR SCHOOL

In our school we hear
Teachers shouting
Pots and pans rattling in the kitchen
People working, playing and singing

When the bell rings the children sing
Then we see them in the class
Finding their homework

The art that we see in the class
And on the posters
The singing coming from the hall

We are very bad at swinging on chairs
And the primary 1s dress up.

Shelley Donaldson (10)
Bankton Primary School

OUR SCHOOL

In our school we hear:
Noisy classrooms
Catty pupils
Moany teachers and
Doors opening

Things we hear:
We hear clattering pots
Going *bang, bang, bang*
Children shouting at one another
And the buzzer from the office
Going *buzz, buzz, buzz*

What are people doing?

People are working hard
People are throwing rubbers
Being silly
And teachers are shouting.

Roxanne Marson (10)
Bankton Primary School

THE DAY THE WINDOW SILL WAS COVERED IN SNOW

The window sill has grown a beard
Grown a beard covered in snow
Glistening in the night as children are running by
Running by in the frosty, bitter night
Anxious to get home in the freezing cold
In the freezing cold, icy pavements are gleaming
In the ferocious night as the snow is punching to the ground
Punching to the ground
Very hard is the ice with the rising wind.

Rachel Gillies (9)
Bankton Primary School

OUR SCHOOL

In our school we see;
The artwork on the walls
Also the classrooms and the doors
The pupils, the teachers and the library

In our school we hear;
People speaking and pots clattering
Toilets being flushed and footsteps in corridors
We also hear pens on whiteboards
And the telephone in the office

In our school people are;
Working hard or not!
Singing in the choir and teachers teaching
Also people are being silly and playing

In our school we are all busy;
Making sounds
Hearing sounds
Doing things.

Ailsa Stryke (10)
Bankton Primary School

OUR SCHOOL

In our school we heard
Telephones and buzzers buzzing at the same time
We heard people talking in the office
In the kitchen we heard pots and pans clashing
I heard Mrs Jamieson and Mrs Talon discussing work
I heard feet hitting on the floor, making loud footsteps
I heard the boiler making funny noises as I went past
I heard people clattering pencils on tables
I heard primary 1s and 2s playing
And I heard teachers giving instructions

In our school I saw posters on the walls
I saw the kitchen with steel shutters on them
I saw shoes and coats hung up
I saw toys in the primary 1's class
I saw the tuck trolley
I saw the clocks on the walls going tick-tock

In our school I saw people being silly
I saw people working hard to try and produce good work
I saw people pinging rubbers around the classroom
I saw people listening well to the teacher
I saw people running about mad
I saw people singing in the GP room.

Graham Gillies (10)
Bankton Primary School

OUR SCHOOL

In our school we hear telephones ringing in the office,
Our assistant head teacher and our head teacher
Discussing out plans for the school,
The buzzer buzzing away until it gets answered,
Footsteps clattering in the corridors,
Our choir singing hymns,
Noises coming from the boiler.

In our school we see blackboards with writing and work
                                        to do on them,
Teachers writing and planning work to do,
Pencils, rulers, rubbers doing their jobs,
Pencils writing, rubbers rubbing and rulers drawing lines,
Clocks and artwork on the wall.

In our school, people are doing work out of text books,
People running and playing in the playground,
People talking and chatting with their pals,
People playing their recorders and making a racket.

Greg Mann (10)
Bankton Primary School

OUR SCHOOL

We can hear . . .
Children and teachers laughing
Pupils flibbertigibbet about each other
Everyone talking about last night's TV
The school bell as we tiredly enter the school

We can see . . .
Artwork on the wall
Special awards
People
Chairs and tables

We are doing . . .
Work
Helping teachers and friends
Thinking about what we are doing after school
Getting into trouble

I smell . . .
Yucky school dinners
Boys' aftershave as they walk past your seat

This is . . .
Our school!

Laura Thomson (11)
Bankton Primary School

GLISTENING SNOW POEM

The window sill has grown a beard
The beard drops silently to the glistening pavement
The pavement was covered in soft white fluffy snow
The soft white fluffy snow has large and small footprints
The large and small footprints were made by people
In the dark icy streets
People in the streets made screeches and screams as the children slid
Straight down the slippery slope
Slopes are covered in soft white snow
Soft fluffy snow is melting as the sun comes out
As the sun came out all the whiteness disappeared
The snow has gone, there's no more snowball fights
The long window sill has no longer got a beard.

Toni Cochrane (10)
Bankton Primary School

OUR SCHOOL

In our school I hear teachers shouting
Pots and pans rattling in the kitchen
People pushing in their chairs
And having a carry-on

In our school the things I see
Are the janitor's office
And the library
And I see cars and buses
And I see the boiler room

In our school people talk
Play and do work
People sing in the choir
And people listen to the teacher.

Dean Stephens (11)
Bankton Primary School

OUR SCHOOL

In our school we can hear . . .
Teachers writing homework with their squeaky pen
People flibbertigibbet about football
I hear the boiler bubbling and gurgling in the boiler room

In our classroom I see . . .
Designed cars driving along the road
I see children laughing and working
Bags scattered along the floor
I see paper everywhere
The teacher's lunch in the pigeon hole

In our school people are . . .
Getting in trouble
Doing work and art
Laughing when someone does something stupid
Filling their bottle with water

I smell . . .
Boys' aftershave as they walk past me
Teachers' perfume
School dinners, yuk!

Kerry Stewart (11)
Bankton Primary School

OUR SCHOOL

In my school I hear . . .

The incomprehensible silence of an empty classroom
The chit-chat conversation in noisy classes
The squeaky footsteps of wet shoes over the floor
The eerie noise of the teacher's shout
But worst of all, the screech-like sound of nails on a blackboard

In my school I see . . .

People continuously talking out of place
Beautifully coloured artwork and masterpieces
The drawings and paintings of pupils' art to disguise the ugly walls

In my school people are . . .

Working hard, not shouting
Biting ready-chipped nails
Joyful pupils singing in the choir
Getting on with the job in hand
Or basically being at school.

Corey Prigmore (11)
Bankton Primary School

BEAUTIFUL BIRDS

One sunny day up in the treetops there were beautiful birds
Beautiful birds were glistening like rainbow colours on their
                                                    long bodies
Their long bodies were shining like diamonds
Like diamonds, their beaks are shimmering like gold
Like gold, their claws sparkle like money
Like money, their eyes sparkle like rubies
Rubies are as precious as all of these birds.

Lois Smith (10)
Bankton Primary School

MY SENSES

Teachers are shouting really loud
Pupils are not listening
'Class, sssh please,' teacher yells
Children in our daydreams

Pencil, rubbers and rulers on our tables
Pictures on walls of happy coats
Green wellie boots with snow on them
Coats on the floor, teacher shouts,
'Put them away'

Bell goes for break
People throwing balls of paper
'Stop that,' helper shouts
'Right,' said children

Chips and chicken drummers on the menu
Sniff that lovely smell
Tummies grumbling saying *I'm so hungry*
Bell rings for lunch
'Yes,' pupils shout

These are my senses.

Ruth Murray (11)
Bankton Primary School

THE PARTY

As I glided down the stairs
In my party dress
My mum said, 'You look beautiful
I know you'll look the best

You look so admirable, brilliant and glamorous
So neat, so lovely and gorgeous
You're pretty, charming and graceful
So cute, superb and irresistible.'

When I got to the disco
I wished that I could go
I saw the school bully
She was *bad* and it did show

She was so vicious, so nasty and cruel
So rotten, beastly and dreadful
Unworthy, wicked and vile
So awful, wrong and a criminal

The time soon came to go
I couldn't wait to get home
I was so *happy* to be here
You'd think I was queen of the throne

I was so ecstatic, overjoyed and delighted
So festive, glad and light-hearted
I felt blissful, lively and cheerful
So please and proud, so gleeful.

Hannah Brownlie (10)
Bankton Primary School

THE PARTY

I was preparing to go to a party
I was dressed up smart
My mum asked, 'What's the matter?'
I replied, 'I've a *worried* heart.'

My heart was anxious, so boomy and troubled
So restless, jumpy and terrified
It was so concerned, afraid, so uneasy
So scared, so frightened and petrified

When I arrived at the party
I believed it was certainly ghouly
When I strolled though the door
I was *shocked* to see a bully

I was so alarmed, so astonished, so staggered
So dumbfounded, so appalled, so amazed
I felt so stunned, surprised and astounded
I was so confused, bewildered and dismayed

The bully marched towards me
My heart was booming like mad
When the bully reached me
I decided to be as *tough* as my dad

I acted so tough, hardy and robust
Hardwearing, beefy and brawny
So powerful, so wiry and durable
I was indestructible, muscular and mighty.

Craig Mahood (10)
Bankton Primary School

THE LITTLE PUPPY

I was strolling through the park
Something caught my eye
It was snow-white and fluffy
It was a *cute* minute puppy

It was endearing, bewitching and fetching
Good-looking, glamorous and tempting
So charming, quaint and captivating
It looked loveable, inviting and fascinating

The puppy was shy and very small
It didn't bite or bark
It wasn't *unpleasant* in any way
But excited and joyful in light and dark

It wasn't vicious, horrid, harsh or frightful
Unfriendly, crude, nasty or spiteful
Not vulgar, grizzly, awful or tough
It wasn't vile, bad tempered, odious or rough

As I watched it frolic in the grass
It looked *happy* and excited and wanted to play
It was running around feeling very glad
It barked at me as if it welcomed me to stay
It was blissful, cheerful, overjoyed, delighted
Festive, elated, glad and excited
So contented, lively, merry and cheerful
It was exuberant, joyful, pleased and gleeful.

Rochelle Fagan (10)
Bankton Primary School

THE BEAST

There was a monster who was hairy
He was planning to dominate Earth
He was incredibly scary
And he believed he was *tough* ever since birth

So durable, hardwearing, so lasting, so indestructible
So beefy, so brawny, so unbreakable
This beast was muscular, hard, strong and strenuous
Also robust, difficult, stiff and laborious

The monster raided our school
He became stunned with shock
He looked like a trouble, petrified ghoul
Who was in a *mad* and idiotic lock

He went berserk, crazy, delirious, demented
Really deranged, dotty, insane and frenzied
So loony, wild and he was a maniac
Unhinged, hysterical and looked like a lunatic

He vaulted through the window
'What a leaper,'
Everyone screamed, 'Wow!'
But still he was as *scary* as the Grim Reaper.

Connel Thompson (10)
Bankton Primary School

BONFIRE NIGHT

I see the fireworks exploding in the air
And glamorous colours in the sky

I smell the aroma of sausages cooking
I smell the aroma of cooking marshmallows
I smell wood burning with rubber

I touch the old, tatty, raggy Guy Fawkes
He is strawy and feathery
I touch a firework not lit

I taste bits of sausages in my mouth
I taste bits of marshmallow, also in my mouth

I hear the echo of fireworks exploding
Children shouting and screaming

I feel a spider climbing up my spine.

Michael Storrie (11)
Bankton Primary School

SNOWY DAYS

The window sill has grown a soft, fluffy beard
A soft beard that glistens in the sun
In the sun I saw people making enormous snowmen
Enormous snowmen wherever you look
Wherever you look children are throwing snowballs
Snowballs are darting to everyone in the street
Everyone in the street laughing and having fun
Having fun in the soft powdered snow
Powdered snow is melted in the boiling sun
The boiling sun melted the soft, fluffy beard.

Stacey Noble (9)
Bankton Primary School

COLOURS

Yellow is as funny as Bart Simpson
As bright as my dad's yellow car
Like yellow golden streetlights
As pretty as a golden sparkling ring

Blue is as beautiful as a summer sky
As stormy as the blue sea
Like my bright blue computer
As bright as a new pencil case

Green is a nice colour
Because it's nice and colourful
As beautiful as a new leaves on a tree
Like a green rolling hill
As green as the beautiful green grass

Red is as gigantic as a London bus
As beautiful as a summer sunset
Like a romantic rose
As bright as nice soft lips.

James Dunn (8)
Bankton Primary School

SNOWDRIFT

Falling from the sky like a comet racing down to Earth
Swirling like a big angry tornado
Bouncing like a big basketball
Drifting like a hairdryer blowing you away
Placing itself onto the ground
Dissolving, going away, just like water going down the plughole.

Edward Watt (11)
Bankton Primary School

DOLPHIN

Its beautiful body glided beside a passing ship
I saw its smooth tail flick as it swam
It jumped and let itself fall into the water

It moved soundlessly through the water
Sometimes noticing a passing fish
I heard it screech to its friends and family
It whirled through the air with an almighty *splash*

It swam to the surface which stopped making it
Look like it could float on water
It plunged over its family member
And fell into the sea
It jumped and twirled in mid-air
And dived into the sea's depths

I'd love to be the animal that I have been describing.

Nicole Hoffie (8)
Bankton Primary School

THE HIDEOUS GIANT

Beth met a hideous giant
A hideous giant with green bulging eyes
With green bulging eyes, that sparkled at night
When they sparkled at night they lit up the world
They lit up the world with a huge bang of thunder
This bang of thunder was the giant's call
The call to Beth to come to his cave
Beth went to his cave and looked around
As she looked around, the giant was watching
Watching from where his three-headed beast was kept.

Bethanie Combe (9)
Bankton Primary School

THE SHIVERING GHOST

There was an old, shivering ghost up in the sky for ten nights,
For ten nights the creepy old ghost woke up all children in the village,
In the village there was an enormous Christmas tree outside the houses,
Outside the houses there was five foot of snow glistening
                                                on pavements,
On the pavements was the old ghost glowing in the dark
                                                and making noises,
Making lots of noise to wake up all the children,
Wake up all the children to scare them to death tonight,
Tonight the shivering ghost is going to destroy the Christmas tree,
The Christmas tree will definitely not be there in the morning,
In the morning there was an old shivering ghost.

Craig Wilson (9)
Bankton Primary School

THE SNOWY WINDOW SILL

The window sill has grown a beard
The beard is soft, fluffy and thick
Fluffy and thick as it glistens in the sun
In the sun people are making patterns of footprints
Footprints in every direction you look
Everywhere you look children are throwing snowballs
Snowballs flying everywhere to anyone you look at
Everyone you look at is covered in soft snow
The snow has melted away till next year
Till next year the snow has disappeared.

Holly Simpson (10)
Bankton Primary School

FIREWORKS

The bonfire sparks spread like bright seeds,
Bright seeds that sparkle on the ground and in the air,
In the air the fireworks went off with a *boom* and a *bang*,
A bang so loud that it made all the other bright colourful
                                    fireworks look incredible,
Boom went the glittering fireworks,
Glittering fireworks were red, ocean-blue, apple-green and
                                    yellow sand colours,
Colours so bright it made people look with their eyes,
Their eyes were filled with excitement,
Excitement to see the rockets,
The rockets went off with a whizz and a magnificent bonfire spark.

Lauren Westwood (9)
Bankton Primary School

CALM AND STORMY

The sea is a hungry dog, giant and grey,
Giant and grey are the rocks upon the seabed,
The seabed is covered by the slashing sea,
The slashing sea leaps up the beach like a leaping tiger,
Like a leaping tiger the sea roars out with rage,
With rage the sea tears apart the towering cliffs,
The towering cliffs look upon the lively sea,
This lively sea turns calm as the sun rises,
The sun rises and winds disappear,
As winds disappear the sea becomes a sleeping baby in your hands.

Christopher Little (9)
Bankton Primary School

COLOURS

Red is like a red, juicy apple
As red as someone's lips
Like a romantic red rose
As beautiful as a sunset on the beach

Blue is like a cold icicle
As blue as my dad's car
Like the blue sea
As bright as the sky

Yellow is as nice as a daffodil
As yellow as Bart Simpson
Like a yellow sandcastle
As hot as the bright sun

Green is the colour of a stem
As fragile as an emerald
Like the colour of the grass
As nice as leaves.

Blair Stryke (8)
Bankton Primary School

THE WINDOW SILL HAS GROWN A BEARD

The window sill has grown a beard
This beard is covered in fluffy white snow
This fluffy white snow as it plunged and fell
Plunged and fell, as it falls to the icy ground
The icy ground lays softly as it lets snow flutter down
Down falls spangling snow as it shines in the golden sunlight
The golden sunlight melts all the whiteness.

Beth Hutchison (9)
Bankton Primary School

Colours

Blue is like a lovely bluebell flower in the summer,
As the big open sky up above our heads,
Like the big blue sea where all the fish live,
As blue as a lovely sapphire.

Silver is like a big crystal ball,
As beautiful as the stars twinkling in the night sky,
Like a sparkling necklace glistening in the light,
As lovely as silver paint on a painting

Green is for a car going as fast as it can
As the green grass goes left and right in the wind
Like a green flower, trying not to move in the wind
Like a green bin that gets rubbish put inside it

Red is for beautiful lips shining in the sunlight
As red as a red rose, smells so nice
Like a pair of lovely, twinkling red shoes
As red paper with a lovely love-heart on it.

Lisa Brownlie (8)
Bankton Primary School

Snow

Dropping like leaves drop off the autumn trees
Twisting and turning as the wind guides it to its destination
Drifting lazily as though it has lost its way down to Earth
Landing softly like soft little balls of bouncy white cotton wool
Lying on the ground like a white blanket of snow covering all
Melting as the sun comes back to life
And rids the land of ice, snow and cold
Snow.

Louise Henderson (11)
Bankton Primary School

COLOURS

Red is like a romantic rose
As beautiful as red rose lips
Like the beautiful sparkling sunset
As bright as people's red blood

Green as a bright pencil case
As juicy as a green pear
Like the lovely smooth grass
As the sweet, falling leaves

Blue is as bright as the sky
As beautiful as the sea
Like the straightness of a lace
As the rain coming down from the sky

Yellow is as bright as the sun
As tasty as butter
Like the sparkling daffodils in the sun
As beautiful as a yellow car.

Lori Nelson (8)
Bankton Primary School

SNOW AND ICE

Falling beautifully from the big blue sky
Swirling like a hundred disco balls clashing
Drifting like a feather from the sky
Sparkling like a thousand diamonds shining in the sun
Laying like a white blanket on Earth
Melting like an ice cream on a cone dropping on my hands
Snow.

Christie Hyde (11)
Bankton Primary School

COLOURS

Red is as brill, pretty and beautiful as a car
As nice as a red strawberry
Like a red piece of paper
As red as night's sunset
As cold as a frog's blood.

Green as the wet grass
As wet as leaves
Like slushy plants
As big as a green box.

Blue is like the summer sky
As big as a book
Like beautiful colours
As blue as pens.

Yellow is as light as a street light
As soft as sand
Like a yellow folder
A yellow car.

Neil Mann (8)
Bankton Primary School

A SNOW POEM

Falling heavily from the sky like tears from someone's eyes,
Swirling like a disco ball,
Drifting like someone carrying a sleigh across the snow,
Glittering like a dancer's dress shining away,
Snow.

Samantha MacLeod (11)
Bankton Primary School

COLOURS

Red is a beautiful rose
Like lovely lipstick
Roses are lovely
As the rose is sitting in the room

Blue is like the beautiful sky
Blue for the sea
The sea has waves
The beautiful sky and sea are lovely

Green for the beautiful grass
The lovely leaves
Green for my brother's room
Green for the paper

Gold is lots of money
The beautiful gold hair
Lots of treasure
Gold for a beautiful gown.

Ashleigh Stephens (8)
Bankton Primary School

SNOW

Plunging like a bungee-jumper falling from the Forth Road Bridge
Zipping like an athlete running for the championship at Sydney
Swirling like a tumble-dryer that thuds the ground over and over again
Chilling like the young lad that leans against the wall
Shining like a dancer's sparkling dress that glitters in the dark night
Thawing like the snow, disintegrated and melting
Snow.

Christopher Tucker (11)
Bankton Primary School

COLOURS

Blue is like a very deep sea
As scary as very big sharks
Like a very blue sky
As beautiful as a summer bluebell

Red is like a beautiful red rose
As beautiful as the red sunset
Like a very fun bouncy ball
As sticky as yummy jam

Yellow is like the very noisy Simpsons
As shiny and beautiful as the sun
Like a bright yellow pencil
As cool as a yellow beetle

Green is as beautiful as a green pen
As green and smooth as grass
Like a very warm tent
As nice as green lipstick.

Jack Thompson (8)
Bankton Primary School

THE LIFE OF SNOW

Collecting in a giant cloud
Big balloon filling up with tiny fractions of air
Plunging lightly down to Earth like icy tears from the sky above
Settling like a big white blanket that covers the surrounding area
Freezing when the air gets colder like a chicken left in the
                                                    freezer too long
Sparkling like so many diamonds scattered across the land
Dissolving when the sun rises and its time is up
Snow.

Ross Fagan (11)
Bankton Primary School

COLOURS

Purple is the colour of my mum's bright room,
As the bright night sky,
Like the boy's bright folder,
As bright as a piece of paper

Yellow is the colour of my sister's bright room,
As bright as the colour of the yellow flowers,
Like the bright sunlight
As bright as the sun

Red is the colour of the roses
As bright as an apple
Like the bright sunset
Red as a nice new car

Blue is like the sea
Blue as an ice cube
Like a bright jacket
As bright as a sapphire.

Chloe Bartlett (8)
Bankton Primary School

SNOW

Falling heavily onto the ground
Turning it white like it's been covered in paint,
Dropping down from the sky to hit the ground,
Plunging down in the big blizzard that covers most of the country,
Dripping from the roofs of houses as it melts,
Drifting across the road in the wind,
Floating in the big puddles,
Snow.

Liam Pace (11)
Bankton Primary School

COLOURS

Blue is a nice jotter
As good as new like a ruler
Like your own nice workbook
As lovely as a blue folder

Red as a romantic rose
As red as a red tray
Like a lovely sunset going down
As red as yucky blood inside bodies

Yellow as the bright sun
As good as Bart Simpson
Like a nice shiny yellow car
As soft as lovely sand.

Sean Durnan (8)
Bankton Primary School

THE MYSTERIOUS NIGHTS

One cold night something happened
Something happened that was mysterious
Mysterious it was until this day
The day it happened it came to stay
It stayed for ten long miserable nights
These nights were extremely scary and terrifying
Scarier and more terrifying than you can ever imagine
Scarier it got every night
Night by night it became more horrifying
But on this eerie day something weird happened.

Christopher McGhee (9)
Bankton Primary School

SNOW

Drifting lightly through the grey sky
Falling and swirling towards the ground

Floating swiftly down onto gardens and trees

Plunging straight onto roofs as it flurries in the wind

Swirling like a disco ball in the wind, way up high

Dipping every time the wind catches it

Crunching under people's feet
Like a big bowl of cornflakes

Snow.

Ross Goodfellow (11)
Bankton Primary School

THE GREAT OLD TREE

Deep in the forest was a great old tree,
The great old tree had wooden-brown and golden-yellow leaves,
Wooden-brown and golden-yellow leaves like a lion roaring
                                              in the wind,
Roaring in the deep dark forest among all the trees,
Among all the trees the great old tree sang,
Sang the tune of Mother Nature deep in the forest
Deep in the forest these trees talked about the Earth
Talking of the Earth and what we could be doing
Doing to help the trees live longer than longer can be
Laughing we will live forever deep in the forest.

Jamie McRoberts (9)
Bankton Primary School

SNOW POEM

Dropping from the sky in small lumps the size of grapes
And going to the ground to make a big white cushion,
Tumbling in the middle of the air like someone tumbling down a hill
And finding a place to land,
Laying on the ground with more snow joining it
And making a white blanket,
Drifting off the ground by the wind like the leaves drifting
off trees in autumn,
Softening on the ground as it is starting to melt,
Evaporating, going away, just disappearing,
Until there is nothing else left but some wet patches on the ground,
Snow.

Rachael Ralston (11)
Bankton Primary School

THE DAY THE SEA WAS VICIOUS

The sea was a hungry dog, giant and grey
Giant and grey are the towering rocks the waves lash upon
Upon the seabed waves crash in with cries of sorrow
Sorrow is what comes when the sailors are washed away
Washed away like a drifting body lifeless and pale
Pale is the colour of the sea when it is resting
Resting like a newborn baby, calm as the sun
As the sun begins to rise, the sea completely settles
As the sea completely settles, the storm is over once again
So the sea is no longer a hungry dog.

Michael McCormick (10)
Bankton Primary School

SNOW POEM

Falling heavily from the sky onto the ground
Forming a layer of white, fluffy stuff
Like the icing on a birthday cake,
Glistening in the midnight sky
As it falls like dancers twirling in their sparkling tutus,
Dripping from the sky like someone crying when they're hurt,
Laying on the ground like a person snuggled in bed
Under a white blanket,
Thawing when it goes slushy, like melting ice cream,
Disappearing when its time is up
Like when rain evaporates when the sun comes out during summer,
Snow.

Erin Bradley (11)
Bankton Primary School

THE NEW YEAR BONFIRE

The bonfire sparks spread like bright seeds,
These bright seeds spread across the dark night-time sky
This night-time sky is filled with dazzling colours
These dazzling colours end with a bang
This bang wakes the sleeping children from their dreams
From their dreams they sit by the window and admire the sky
The sky was lit up with the bonfire sparklers
Welcome to Bonfire Night.

Stephen McCutcheon (9)
Bankton Primary School

COLOURS

Red is like lovely glittery new nail varnish
As bright as a red romantic rose
Like a big beautiful strawberry
As bright as red lipstick

Blue is like a big school jotter
As lovely as the blue sky
Like the big splashes of rain
As blue and big as the ocean

Green is like a big juicy apple
As green as a big fat pepper
Like a scrunched-up leaf
As big as a pear

Yellow is as bright as light
As pretty as the sun
Like a lovely big sunflower
As yellow as the sand.

Stacey Linney (8)
Bankton Primary School

SNOW

Plunging as it darts down from the sky above,
Swirling like a spinning top racing down to Earth,
Bouncing like a ball hitting off a surface,
Drifting like a feather from the sky,
Flying like a white blanket on the ground,
Melting like it's starting all over again.

Blayre Currie (11)
Bankton Primary School

COLOURS

Red is as bright and as light as blood
As red and as dark as jam
Like a very big and bright ball
As light as a very bright red pen

Blue is as bright as a book
As bright and as light as a carpet
Like a bright blob of paint
As big as a bright blue pencil

Green is really bright grass
As green as a gigantic robot
Like a big clump of hair
As big as a fat rubber

Yellow is as heavy as a car
As yellow as a big bit of ice cream
Like a gigantic piece of cardboard
As fantastic as my big bedcover!

Benjamin Snodgrass (8)
Bankton Primary School

COLOURS

Red is like a beautiful romantic rose
As bright as a person's lovely red blood
Like the beautiful sparkly sunset
As juicy as a big strawberry

Blue is like the beautiful sky above
As big and long as the sea
Like the rain coming down from the sky
As straight as a lake

Green is as lovely as the grass
As sweet as falling leaves
Like a sweet, tasty apple
As hairy as lots of pears

Gold is like pretty rings
As beautiful as earrings
Like pointy-shaped diamonds
As long as Barbie's and Rapunzel's golden hair.

Kerry-ann Symington (8)
Bankton Primary School

THE TREE SHEPHERD

Once there was a great elderly tree
The great elderly tree was proud and strong
Strong and proud it walked the Earth
The Earth's trees is what it looked after
It looked after the trees amazingly
Amazingly it magically covered the ground
The ground turned green and trees came alive
Coming alive and sounding the horns of Mother Nature
Mother Nature sang for these sacred trees
Sacred trees that shall last forever.

Aaron Galvin (9)
Bankton Primary School

APE

Apes with their black noses and brown warm fur
Apes with a fierce face
Apes with a fierce roar
Apes with their angry shout, makes the jungle shake
Apes swing from tree to tree
Apes could climb the highest tree man has ever seen
Apes crawl on the knuckles of their hands
Apes are so strong, like a macho man
I wish I could be like an ape
I wish I could be . . .
I wish I could be . . .

Alastair Stirrat (8)
Bankton Primary School

THE SCARY WOLF

Deep in the forest there was an old, black wolf
An old black wolf with green creepy eyes
Green creepy eyes that glistened brightly in the midnight sky
In the midnight sky he howled at the bright full moon
The bright full moon was getting darker with clouds slowly
                                approaching over the dark sky,
Over the dark sky was clouds shaped like demons, mad and creepy
Mad and creepy, they were watching you all night
All night the wolf hunts in the deep dark forest.

Ben Harman (10)
Bankton Primary School

I FELL ASLEEP IN CLASS TODAY

I fell asleep in class today,
As I was awfully bored.
I laid my head upon my desk
And closed my eyes and snored.

I woke to find a piece of paper
Stuck to my face.
I'd slobbered on my text books
And my hair was a disgrace.

My clothes were badly rumpled
And my eye were glazed and red.
My binder left a three-ring
Indentation on my head.

I slept through class
And probably would have slept some more,
Except my classmates woke me,
As they headed out the door.

Carrie Burnett (10)
Blackridge Primary School

A GARDEN OF FLOWERS

A garden of flowers is a wonderful place,
Especially in summer and spring,
You can do anything you want to do,
Doesn't matter if you get a sting.

It's just so full of lovely colours,
Red, pink and blue,
You might spot some orange and purple
Sneaking around there too.

There's just so many varieties of flowers,
All on one spot of grass,
Roses, violets, tulips and more,
You can't help look as you pass.

When they've only just been planted,
It looks so boring there,
But when they sprout to reach the sky,
Oh how they look so fair.

But you better watch out that nobody steals
A flower from this wonderful place,
Because if they do, what you'll be left with is
One big empty space.

So out of ten, I'll give it nine
And that's quite a good score,
For a mere bunch of planted seeds,
Lying outside someone's door.

Carrie Leighann Boardman (10)
Blackridge Primary School

FRIENDS TILL THE END

If you're ever in trouble,
I'll be there for you
And do you promise you'll be there for me too?

'Cause if you do, we'll be . . .
Friends till the end!

If you're ever in a jam,
Here I am,
We'll stick together like a sheep and a lamb.

'Cause if you do, we'll be . . .
Friends till the end!

We go together like carrots and peas
And when we go out,
We get dirty knees.

'Cause if you do, we'll be . . .
Friends till the end!

If you ever feel so angry, you land in jail,
I'm your bail,
'Cause we are the friendship boat with the big high sail.

'Cause if you do, we'll be . . .
Friends till the end!

If you're ever down a well,
Ring my bell,
If you're ever up a tree,
Phone for me.

'Cause we'll always be . . .
Friends till the end!

Rachel Craig (10)
Blackridge Primary School

MY ROOM

My room is messy
My room is dark
Open the door and see my shark
Go under my bed
And guess what you'll see?
A hairy monkey *oooaaaeee*
Go in my wardrobe
Behind my clothes and see
My toes
Go in my dryer
And see my socks *pooeee!*
On top of my wardrobe
Teddy bears lie, they walk and talk
But never die.

Martin Caldwell (10)
Letham Primary School

MARY'S POEM

Mary, Mary
Contrary
Light as snow
Snow flows
Mary blows
Tickles inside her toes
Mary goes
To the shows
Blows with the wind
And was never
Seen again.

Scott Bates (11)
Letham Primary School

My Room

My room is nice and warm
It's got a PlayStation, video and TV
No animals, no noises
The bed is nice and cuddly

So very quiet in my room
You won't feel a bit of cold
You won't be disturbed
I have lots of toys that won't get sold.

Daniel McGuckin (11)
Letham Primary School

Cheat

Leanne went for Gemma, knocked on her door,
Jamie went for Paul, knocked on the door,
They go down to the park,
To play rounders in the dark,
A light came on,
So they shouted, 'Go on.'
Paul dropped the bat
And ran to the first mat,
'You cheat, you stopped and ran!' everyone shouted.
'So, who said I ran?'
'Everyone! Even that man.'
'I saw that you stopped and ran,' said the man.

'Cheat! Cheat!'

Leanne Temple (11)
Springfield Primary School

WINTER

I pull back the curtains
The world has changed!
White and silent, a thick white blanket,
Silencing the land.
A set of delicate prints left by a robin
Are the only things to have disturbed the whiteness.
Everything is quiet, silent and peaceful,
Waiting for another blizzard to begin
And disturb the deep drifts.

Louisa Brown (11)
Springfield Primary School

THE LAST LEAVES

Red, orange and brown,
The colours of the last leaves
Lie still on the ground.
A wind will blow them away
As winter returns.

Andrew Cochrane (11)
Springfield Primary School

WINTER

The snow falls as gently as can be,
I go outside and have a snowball fight,
Then more snow falls as I go inside,
I watch it fall on the ground,
It glitters on the grass like diamonds.

Sarah Litster (11)
Springfield Primary School

MY DOG, PELE!

My dog, Pele,
He never liked jelly,
We were always together,
Whenever, whatever,
Then one day he turned
Like an icicle,
He could never run
With me on my bicycle,
I miss my dog,
I really do,
I just wish he was here,
With me and you!

Lisa Greig (11)
Springfield Primary School

WINTER

Winter is the time of year
When snowflakes fall
And trees are bare.

White snow all over the place,
You can't see the ground,
Not a trace.

Snowball fights happening,
Children playing and laughing,
The beautiful snowflakes on the ground,
Everyone playing all around!

Kathryn Swanson (11)
Springfield Primary School

TOM'S NEW BIKE

It was Tom's birthday,
On the Thursday.
He got a bike,
He really did like.
'Mommy, look at this,' cried Tom.
'Oh, it is lovely,' answered Mom.

He took it to school one day,
He rode it all the way.
All his friends had a shot on it,
This made them very fit.
A bully said, 'You'll be sad,
If I can't have a shot on your bike, young lad.'

He walked home that day,
Sulking all the way.
'Where is your bike?' asked Kay.
'The bully, he took it away!'

Kathryn Nieuwstadt (11)
Springfield Primary School

WINTER

The frost is glittering on the ground,
The snowman stands without a sound,
The feathers swirl round and round,
The icy wind batters, noisy like a hound,
Everybody outside having fun,
Now the sun has come to say hello,
The snowman is so low, it has melted.

Gillian Scott (11)
Springfield Primary School

WINTER

I looked out of the window, snowflakes trickled to the ground
The robins were singing, what a lovely sound
The bells were ringing
It was Christmas Day
I leapt with joy, hip hip hooray!
I ran down the stairs and opened the door
To find the toys all over the floor
I opened them up one by one
And I showed them all to my mum
I wrapped up warm and went outside
And I had lots and lots of snowball fights
It was time to come in
Because it was getting dim
I went in and played with my new game, The Sims.

Hazel McCartney (11)
Springfield Primary School

WINTER

The snow falls softly on the ground,
It falls down gently, not making a sound.
The children play, all having fun.
They play until day is nearly done.
Children having snowball fights
And staring at the pretty Christmas lights.
For Christmas Eve is nearly here
And Santa Claus will drink his beer!

Rachael Doherty (11)
Springfield Primary School

THE BULLY

Oh no! It's Monday again and time for school,
The bully is bound to make me out to be a fool,
Oh why can't she just be kind?
If she was nice, I wouldn't mind!

Always snapping, snipping, snarling
And giving her classmates a good kicking,
The bully pays scant attention
To the school rules and isn't scared by the odd detention.

I can never stand up to her when she hits,
The other day she stole my best mitts,
Yesterday she stole Becky's coat,
Today she had Simon by the throat.

None of us like this school anymore,
The bully's antics have become such a bore.
She thinks she's super cool,
But we think she is a prize fool.

We've just had our best Monday,
I suppose it was going to happen one day,
A new boy started this morning,
His name is Morgan and he's our Prince Charming.

Now we are no longer bullied or sad,
Morgan has put the bully firmly in her place.
He's not scared of the bully's threats,
Now the bully has many regrets!

Natasha Black (11)
Springfield Primary School

THE WINTER'S DAY

Drip, drop!
went the snowflakes on a cold and frosty morning.

Crickle, crackle!
went the sitting room fire.

Whoosh, shoo!
went the cold morning breeze.

Crack, crickle!
went the ice as it split in two.

Bang, splurge!
went the snowball as it hit the child's jacket.

Yawn, zzzz!
went the old man, napping at the end of a winter's day.

Scott Noon (11)
Springfield Primary School

WINTER POEM

Snowflakes falling gently to the ground,
Not even making one single sound.
Then everything is covered in white,
What a beautiful sight!
Children playing and having fun,
Giggles and laughter from everyone.
But night occurs and we go to bed,
With dreams of playing in the snow in our heads.

Ailie McClay (11)
Springfield Primary School

THE CATHERINE WHEEL

Whizzing, whizzing round the catherine wheel goes,
It starts off slow and whistles more
And louder than ever before.
Whizzing, whizzing round it goes,
Its pretty colours on show.
Whizzing, whizzing, round it goes,
It starts to slow, oh no!
Whizzing, whizzing round it goes,
It stopped, what a shame.
It doesn't go round and round,
No, not now, not ever again.

Katie Turnbull (11)
Springfield Primary School

007 WANNA-BE!

I've always wanted to be a secret agent like 007 on TV,
I know I don't look like him but that won't put off me,
I'd like to drive fast sports cars and spend most of my time in pubs,
I would take up gambling and drinking vodka Martinis.

As soon as my mum and dad stopped being meanies,
I would be able to pursue my dreams as 'diamonds are forever'.
As long as I 'died another day',
'The world will never be enough'.

Alexander Chadwick (11)
Springfield Primary School

THE HOUSE

The house opens its eyes to a new morning,
It opens its eyes slowly,
The house has watery eyes as the shower goes on,
It blinks as the lights go on,
The toaster swallowed up the toast
And then spits it back out,
The bowl munches up the cereal and drinks the milk,
The house gargles as I brush my teeth,
The house is warmed by the sun,
The letter box gobbles up the post,
The teeth open as a visitor comes in,
The house stares at me as I leave for school.

Scott Fyfe (11)
Springfield Primary School

WINTER POEM

Fawns grazing in the meadows and the frosty grasses
Does watching as the winter season passes
The stag has gone, gone out hunting
She's feeling lonely as the hogs aren't grunting
Then suddenly she hears the pull of a trigger
And in the meantime a sinister snigger
The fawn falls with its knees knocking
How could she present this news so shocking?
As the seasons go on and on
Still in remembrance of that poor little fawn.

Ross Shepherd (11)
Springfield Primary School

SNOWFLAKES POEM

Snowflakes glisten down and down,
People smiling with lots of glee,
Children playing like dogs in the snow,
Their cheeks are so red, like Rudolph's nose,
So cold and happy as they shiver in the snow.

Stuart Grant (11)
Springfield Primary School

WINTER

Winter is the time of year,
For people to jump up and cheer,
Christmas is just round the bend,
With Santa and his jolly friends,
Snow is falling, snowflakes spinning round and round,
Then they cascade to the ground.

Kirsten Trayner (10)
Springfield Primary School

SNOW FALLS

Winter's here, cold, dark night,
Snow falls gently down on the road,
People shiver, chitter and wonder
Whether winter will ever end.
Slippery roads, slippery paths,
Be careful in case you slide.
Woolly hats, scarves and gloves,
Big, thick socks and lovely warm fires.

Lisa Hunter (11)
Springfield Primary School

THE FLEA CIRCUS

Havoc through houses,
Terror through towns,
Here comes the flea circus,
With beetles as clowns.

The bird tamers are worms,
The trapeze artists, ants,
No wonder the trainers
Keep scratching their pants.

For the big finale,
Out come the wings
Of a beautiful butterfly,
That colourfully sings.

On the whole, the applause
From the bug audience
Is capitalised
As the biggest roar since.

They leave the city,
With colossal applause,
They'll be touring the world,
Going round without pause.

Andrew Blythe (10)
Springfield Primary School

WINTER

On that morning, I stood and stared,
When I opened my curtains
And the trees were bare,
Snowflakes falling,
Birds singing,
The children are playing,
The trees are swaying,
Kids are all around,
Making angel shapes on the ground.

Iain Grant (11)
Springfield Primary School

FOOTBALL'S SO GREAT

Oh! I wish I could go out and play,
I hate being stuck inside all day,
Football, that is the game for me,
Running about keeps me fit you see.

On with my top, on with my shorts,
Football boots and my socks,
Running around on the grass pitch,
Playing well, without a hitch.

Ten of my pals play on my team,
Our colours are mostly red, blue and cream,
Ninety minutes of running around,
Football, the game that's sound.

Callum Walker (11)
Toronto Primary School

FOR ZARA

You filled my days with fun and game
You loved playing hide-and-seek
I had to try
To hide your eyes
So you wouldn't peek

You protected me
From danger
With your loud bark
But you were
Always friendly
When we played in the park

You always had
A sweet tooth
For goodies that I ate
You were a kind, loving friend
That's what made you great!

You are no longer with us
Which made me fall apart
But when I think of you
It warms my lonely heart.

Hannah Stirling (11)
Toronto Primary School

LIVING WORLD

Our world is alive,
Every towering green tree,
Every shimmering blue sea
Is bursting with light and life.

We depend on this world of forests and rivers,
Of giant sleeping mountains, dozing peacefully,
But we the supposed intelligent ones -
Are not contented with this garden of Eden.

So we bring our metal monsters, ugly and cruel,
Cutting down forests for our fuel,
Destroying this world with our world of hate and greed,
But we never have time to replant a seed.

Look out your window, can you honestly say
Is that world green or is it grey?

Rosie Smeaton (11)
Toronto Primary School

MY PET HAMSTER

I have a pet hamster called Snowball
I hold her six times a day
Her cage is green and purple
And her birthday is the fourteenth of May.

I love my little pet hamster
Except for once every night
When she plays on her noisy wheel
And wakes me up with a fright.

Aleisha Evans (11)
Toronto Primary School

GRAN

Ageing fast
Forgetting the past
She's boogieing down
With the fogies from town
That's my gran!
I'm her number 1 fan!

Her scones and cakes
Turn out a treat
Can't wait to visit
Her each week
That's my gran!
I'm her number 1 fan!

I sleep over
When Mum and Dad go out
Gran's not like Mum
She doesn't shout
That's my gran!
I'm her number 1 fan!

Her guard dog, Lucy
Is more of a wussy
She likes her grub
But she's a bit of a chub
My gran loves her
And that's all that matters
That's my gran!
I'm her number 1 fan!

Kirsty Kilfeather (10)
Toronto Primary School

DANCE

Every week I go to a hall
And when I'm there, I have a ball
The suit I wear is black and long
And the shoes on my feet are low but strong
I move around from space to space
And try my best to keep the pace
And even though it's not a race
The sweat still runs down my face.

As minutes tick away
I shake from side to side and sway
It can be hard from time to time
But the choice was made and it was mine
I had to take the chance because I want to dance
Dancing is fun for everyone
And if you want to be fit
Then you should come

I bounce and twirl and jump and run
But most of all I have great fun!

Rachel Scoular (11)
Toronto Primary School

THE WORST FOOTBALL TEAM

The worst football team is a soft shooting team,
The team is called the Losers 99,
The reason why they're called this is
Because they never win their games,
Would you like to join that team?

With only 17 fans watching the game
And a bit of stadium filling, they should be ashamed,
The fans only go because the prices are low,
Would you like to join that team?

They're not a fast-running, glory-hunting team,
Would you want to know the colour of their strip?
It is blue, purple, orange and green,
Would you like to join that team?

Saqib Iqbal (11)
Toronto Primary School

MY MESS I CALL A ROOM

If you venture in my room,
You need a compass and a map to find your way out,
My mum and dad, they always say, 'Go clean up your room!'
But I just say, 'I can't find the broom.'
I went to find the Hoover and that I couldn't find,
I went to find the polish and I thought, oh never mind!
I went and told my mum and she just moaned at me,
She told me to go up to my room and stay there till my tea,
So my room still looks like a dump today,
So since I'm grounded with nothing to do,
I think I'll tidy it up today – maybe!

Christopher Robertson (11)
Toronto Primary School

FAT CAT

There once was a fat cat from Japan
Who drove a white Mini van,
He ate Chinese foods,
In all kinds of moods
And lay in the sun with a tan.

There was a fat cat called Tinger
Who thought he was a super singer,
He smelt of raw fish
And cheese in a dish
And often got called a minger.

There was a fat cat that sold mats,
He liked to buy bright yellow hats,
He would put on his shoes
And sing out the blues
And go to find his cute lady cats.

Samantha Wardlaw (11)
Toronto Primary School

CAVIES GALORE

There were two cavies from France
Who learned to hula-hula dance
They tripped on their skirts
When trying to flirt
And now they can't dance for pants!

There were two cavies from Peru
Who wanted to build a canoe
They fell in the river
And learned with a shiver
They hadn't used waterproof glue!

Naomi Young (11)
Toronto Primary School

My Mum

She is cool, hip and funky,
She reminds me of a cute little monkey.
She gets a bit stressed,
When she has to pick up the mess.

She's a great swimmer,
I think she's a winner.
She's an excellent listener
And when she goes away, I miss her.

She has a big heart,
She shops in the Wal-Mart.
She dresses lovely,
Because she's my mummy.

Dawn Balfour (11)
Toronto Primary School

My Holiday

I was going on holiday,
Off to France to play.
'How shall we travel?' Mother asked.
'An aeroplane!' I said.
'We'll fly up high into the sky,
All the way to France.
When we get there, we can chance
And eat French food.'

Working quickly, we pitched the tent
And off to the beach I went.
I splashed and played and swam,
'Croissant s'il vous plait, Madame!'

Duncan Ewing (9)
Torphichen Primary School

SCHOOL IS COOL AND VERY NOISY

School is cool and very noisy,
There's pencils scribbling, teachers talking,
Rulers ruling, rubbers rubbing,
Trays falling, opening, closing,
Children chattering, bells ringing,
Yellow cards flying, pupils crying,
That is just why school is noisy,
School is cool, cool is yet to come.

School is cool, there's teachers teaching,
Television televisioning,
Assemblies assembling, paintbrushes painting,
Chains falling at home time,
Snow days, no school,
Outside is cool, the mound is crumbling,
Snowballs coming, sun is bright as ever,
Lines forming as the bell rings.

The very last bell, the home time bell
Is the best of all because it's time to go home, yippee!

Callum Anderson (9)
Torphichen Primary School

MY ROOM

It's Monday and my room is tired,
until my alarm is then required.
I lie down, just about sleeping,
until my alarm drives me mad beeping.

It's Tuesday and my room is warm,
since my cat slept in it, until dawn.
I lie down, just about sleeping,
until my alarm drives me mad beeping.

It's Wednesday and my room is bored,
for it isn't watching me, playing with my sword.
I lie down, just about sleeping,
until my alarm drives me mad beeping.

It's Thursday and while I'm in bed,
my room is scared about what's ahead.
I lie down, just about sleeping,
until my alarm drives me mad beeping.

It's Friday and my room is glad,
for after school I can be bad.
I wake up, happy and cheerful
and after all, that's what I'm here for.

It's Saturday and my room is cheery
and so am I, today I'm never weary.
I get up, full of joy
and I'm also glad that I'm a boy.

It's Sunday and my room is resting,
watching the builders do their testing.
I lie down, going to sleep
and the good thing is, my alarm won't beep!

Richard Bartlett (11)
Torphichen Primary School

SOME ANIMALS

Animals are wonderful
In all kinds of ways,
Some animals are nasty,
Some are nice.

Sometimes you get cute animals,
Sometimes you get ugly ones.

Some animals are loud,
Some are quiet,
Some have long hair,
Some don't.

Some are big,
Some are small,
Some are large,
Some are wide,
Some are tiny,
Some are gigantic.

Some have no hair,
Some have tons,
Some have curly hair
And some have straight,
Some are fat,
Some are skinny,
Animals are wonderful things.

Raina Gillon (10)
Torphichen Primary School

HORSE LOVE

I have a horse
He is very hard to keep
In the morning I just weep
It's so cold!
He pushes me with his muzzle
And leaves me very puzzled

I pull his mane
But that's a pain
So I put on his rug
And stand there and tug
Then I put him out to graze
In a maze, *oh no!*

I take him in to ride
And make him stride
He tries to gallop
So I give him a wallop
As I waddle
In the saddle
I put on my hat
Then I go *splat, oh no!*

So I go home, annoyed
And try hard to avoid
Then I hear noises
Yes horses! *Oh no!*

Emma Thacker (10)
Torphichen Primary School

SEASHORE

The seashore is a great place to be,
listening to the rough, roaring sea.
The pebbles gleam in the hot sunshine,
while girls and boys have a lovely time.

People lying on the boiling sand,
while seals look at them on the cool land.
Water splashing onto the hot beach,
then with fright the children drop their peach.

Now with their animals they come,
with brothers and sisters and Dad and Mum.
The kids caught some strange looking fishes,
while Mum and Dad put out the dishes.

Now came the new bucket and spade,
then the boiling sun began to fade.
So they gathered everything up
and they went back home to their small pup.

Megan Kavanagh (10)
Torphichen Primary School

MY FEARS

My fear is of monsters that lurk behind the door
My fear is of spiders that creep along the floor
My fear is of aliens that come from outer space
My fear is of darkness, so empty with no face
My fear is of snakes that are at the bottom of my bed
My fear is of ghosts that live out in the shed
My fear is of witches that eat human brains
My fear is of shadows that frighten all the wains.

Tabitha Ewing (11)
Torphichen Primary School

MY HOLIDAY

When the plane left the airport
I started to excite
I saw the sun then it turned bright
The flight turned bumpy
And I was jumpy

When we arrived we got a bus
It was very, very warm
And very, very crushed
It had a guide who never, ever hides

After we unpacked, we went down to the pool
One was very warm, one was very cool
After we had done, we said, 'That was fun!'

We went down to the seaside
Just in time to see the tide
I thought I saw tweed
But it was just some little seaweed

I went on a tour with my dad and my mum
We arrived back and people knew we had come
I said that it was fun and I had a bun

When we went home, I went straight to bed
I then had a dream about painting the hotel red.

Liam Russell (11)
Torphichen Primary School

MY LITTLE PUPPY

I took my little puppy,
To the grass where it was mucky.
We played, jumped, danced and fell
And came back with a smell.
All my mum could say was,
'Tut, tut, tut,' to my little puppy and me.

Soon it was lunchtime
And we went to make some food,
Then my puppy jumped up to me
And stole a little meat,
All my mum could say was,
'Tut, tut, tut,' to my little puppy and me.

'Time for a bath,' Mum called to us,
Then we ran into the bathroom.
We splashed, played, then rolled around
And lots of water went on the ground.
My mum came in to see us,
Then slipped on all the water
And said, 'Tut, tut, tut,' to me and my little puppy.

'Time to go to bed,' Mum called,
So we ran into the bedroom
And fell asleep in no time,
So we could do it all again tomorrow.

Natalie Rigby (10)
Torphichen Primary School

FUN SEASONS

Summer's hot and sunny,
Bees are making honey.
People get a suntan,
Here comes the ice cream van.
Children play in the sand,
While watching the bandstand.
Summer is just wonderful.

Autumn's cool and windy,
Girls play with their Sindy,
But don't worry, you can still have fun,
Even though there is no sun.
Jumping in leaves makes children laugh,
Nothing about autumn is naff.
Autumn is just wonderful.

Winter's cold and snowy,
Sometimes even blowy.
Children make their own snowman,
While mums cook inside with a pan.
Christmas time's coming, so you have to be good,
Or that means no Christmas pud.
Winter is just wonderful.

Spring's when plants start to grow,
There isn't even any snow.
Birds lay eggs in their nests,
They think children are little pests.
Baby lambs run round and round,
Making little bleating sounds.
Spring is just wonderful.

Imogen Beck (8)
Torphichen Primary School

MY ROOM

My room is a mess
A really big mess
Sometimes I can't find my own dress
So really my room is a mess

My room is untidy
So is the jumbly bed
My mum nearly falls dead
So really my room is a mess

My room is cluttered
With all the toys in the place
It's very hard to have a race
So really my room is a mess

My room is not tidy
I have tried to tidy it up
Sometimes I lose my cup
So really my room is a mess

My room looks horrible
I look at it, it looks OK
That can change in a day
So really my room is a mess

My room is now tidy
Because after that year
Mum thinks I'm a dear
And now my room is mostly clear.

Heather Wolfe (8)
Torphichen Primary School

POP STARS

Pop stars are on posters, covered with glitter
They sing, dance and play different instruments
Many people want to see them
So they book a babysitter

Pop stars have fancy cars, probably a limousine
They take very good care of them
They keep them shiny and clean

Pop stars have money, lots and lots
Pop stars need guitars and things so they go to lots of shops

When pop stars are heading onto the big stage
The people in the crowd cheer and rage

When the pop star's voice flies out of the speaker
The boys applaud and the girls get weaker

Pop stars wear crazy wigs and very weird hats
When they get in front of the crowd, the crowd cheer and clap

Pop stars play the guitar and maybe the drum
When you're watching them it is great, great fun!

Alice Gunn (10)
Torphichen Primary School

The Living World

The world is so close to us,
We don't notice it,
There are so many places,
We will never visit.

From the great sandy pyramids,
To the green Amazon forest,
From the vast Sahara Desert,
To the huge Niagara Falls,
From the totally deserted ice regions,
To the overpopulated cities.

The world is so close,
But yet it is so far.
Some people haven't seen the Earth,
But they venture into space.

The world is so close to us,
We don't notice it.
There are so many places,
We will never visit.

Callum Nisbet (11)
Torphichen Primary School

THE FARM

Spring,
The lambing comes that means it's spring,
The streams run and the trees are green,
That's a farmer's year.
Summer,
In the summer the lambing stops
And the gates are opened,
Burling summer tractors cut the grass in the field,
They're put into big round bales,
After that they're wrapped in rubber all during summer,
That's a farm's year.
The fences divide cattle and sheep from the growing grass
That's a farm's year.
Autumn,
During autumn the cows are put in sheds,
The bulls in a pen,
That's a farm's year.
Winter,
The farmer puts bales of straw in the sheds with his tractor,
They're fed and strawed by the farmer
Who led a very busy year.
That's a year in the life of a farmer.

Sam Mitchell (11)
Torphichen Primary School

MY DREAMS

My dream is of journeys to faraway lands,
My dream is of having my own fashion brands.

My dream is of being a celebrity cook,
My dream is of writing the best-selling book

My dream is of having a nice kind of brother,
My dream is of having a fairy godmother.

My dream is of having a sweetie selection,
My dream is of having a perfume collection.

My dream is of having beautiful hair,
My dream is of owning a fierce grizzly bear.

But these are all dreams in my empty head,
As I lie asleep on my feather bed.

Pamela Nisbet (11)
Torphichen Primary School

SILLY BILLY BEE

Silly Billy Bee was a very silly bee,
That silly little bee, named Silly Billy Bee
Never obeyed Honey Bunny King Bee's orders at all.
Silly Billy Bee made Honey Bunny King Bee very angry.
Instead of making honey he annoyed Sally Bee.

Then he even hurt Honey Bunny King Bee with a ball,
Everyone told him he was in *big* trouble.
Honey Bunny King Bee gave Silly Billy one more chance.
If he blew it, he would be out of the Honey Bunny Bee swarm,
From then on, Silly Billy Bee was on his best behaviour,
Silly Billy Bee was no longer silly!

Scott Lister (9)
Torphichen Primary School

THE CHANGING ENVIRONMENT

Leaves on the trees, red, gold, orange
Blackberries ripe on the bush
Need a fire blazing hot
Keeps you warm at night
Sky clear day and night
Spring is nice

Summer weather brings building bricks
Summer brings landscapers
The dumpers come with lots of muck
It is mayhem on the site
The foundations go in
The work has begun . . .

The moving begins
I want my old quietness
I better find a new place
Far away from buildings
I see signs for new houses
Here we go again.

Robbie Compton (9)
Whitdale Primary School

MY FOREST

I lived in an unspoilt land for a long time,
I had fun when I was growing up,
A building site became a city,
I moved away from the place where the site was,
I met new pals there, played with them all day long,
For sale sign up in the forest,
Houses built among the woodland,
New cars moving in.

Craig Forrest (9)
Whitdale Primary School

OUR ENVIRONMENT

Trees rustling from side to side
Birds whistling in the sun
Bees looking for honey
Butterflies laying their eggs
Flowers growing from their roots

Things getting built around the house
Trees getting chopped down
Lots of houses around and about
Flowers dying very quickly
Animals have nowhere to live

Shops getting built around the house
A big circus in the town
Our environment is getting destroyed
Thinking of moving to a better place
Moving into a little cottage, a lovely place.

Jordon Wilkinson (9)
Whitdale Primary School

DESTRUCTION OF THE FOREST

In the forest there were trees rustling,
The birds cheeping,
The sun shining,
The water gently dripping off the trees,
I think one day this will change.

The years passed,
Cars on the road were swooping past,
Buildings were being built very fast,
Quickly, hundreds of people were walking past,
It is changing now.

Soon all of the buildings were complete,
Lots of trucks and cars drove past,
Swiftly and slow,
I will move to a place where trees breathe,
Also to a better landscape.

James Russell (9)
Whitdale Primary School

DESTROYING THE QUIETNESS!

Summery breeze catching leaves
Dewdrops are sweetly shimmering
Birds have not a care in the world
Nice soft grass is shuffling

Noisy tractors driving into trees
People destroying wildlife
New houses getting built
I can't get a wink of sleep

Now there is a giant city
They destroyed the peace and quiet
Cities are noisy places, the sound of horns
I think I will move.

Kate Cartwright (9)
Whitdale Primary School

THE VIEW FROM MY WINDOW

Birds leaping from one branch to another
Leaves swooping across the grass
People walking silently
Sheds creaking

Building getting noisy
People moving in
Diggers digging in the ground
People moving in

Shops and factories getting built
I am twenty now
It's time to move out
I'm getting a new house.

Grant Walker (9)
Whitdale Primary School

THE LANDSCAPE FROM MY WINDOW

Cars zooming along the road,
Trees glistening, snow falling off,
Cars skidding and crashing,
Snow crunching,
Fences blowing, breaking to pieces.

Outside my gran's house,
Trees swishing side to side,
People out playing, throwing snowballs,
People walking up the street,
Footprints in the snow.

Outside my house,
Birds singing so sweetly,
People laying on the snow making angels,
Girls and boys making snowmen,
Me and my friend playing in the snow,
Laura and my mum flinging snowballs.

Ashleigh Smith (9)
Whitdale Primary School

THE BUILDING WORK

Sun is shining, birds are singing,
Grass moving side to side,
Bees are buzzing, lovely beautiful trees,
Nothing is better than my garden.

Some houses are building up,
People digging, people need some help,
Lots of hammering, I hate this noise,
Now everything is changing.

There was a whole entire city,
With giant people shouting, playing, eating,
I really hate this, why are they doing this?
That is it, I can't take it anymore,
We are moving somewhere peaceful and beautiful.

James Ashworth (9)
Whitdale Primary School

OUT OF MY WINDOW

Birds looking for food
Leaving soft gentle footsteps on the snow
Peaceful and quiet stroll
A quiet walk along the grass

Lovely country house getting destroyed
Not very nice, too noisy and spoilt
I don't like it here anymore

So it's time to move, to leave my house
Go away again to peace and quiet
I have to go.

Laura Jane Wood (9)
Whitdale Primary School

From My Window I Can See

From my window I can see blooming trees
And dazzling flowers here and there
Birds singing ever so sweet high, high in the tree tops above
Bright green grass and light pink blossom in the bushes
Rabbits and robins everywhere
I wish that it would stay like this forever
Someday, not for a long, long time, this will all change.

Now from my window I can see diggers, builders
                                and bricks everywhere
Every month and every week a new house, no matter what we do
It's very, very noisy now that there's a road right outside
People having parties every night
There's no birds or trees left now that everything has been cut down
I can't stand the sound of people screaming all night

Oh no, I can't stand this sound
There's no more green land left to play in
There's only houses everywhere
Hammers banging all night long
Metal bars going *clink, clank*
I can't stand this sound
I think I'll move to the countryside.

Hayley Wright (9)
Whitdale Primary School

OUTSIDE THE HOUSE

Trees standing in the breeze
Buttercups twinkling in the sun
The sun burning the skin of a young boy
People sunbathing on the beach
Bees fluttering in the sky

Trucks carrying sand
People hammering hammers on wood
Diggers digging holes, making a path
Men chopping down trees
People shouting on poles

People living in houses, having parties
Houses, flats, shops in the way
Moving truck came, all the stuff went away
Move away to a cottage and look at the trees
For sale signs going up, building trucks came.

Sara McIntosh (9)
Whitdale Primary School

LOOKING THROUGH THE WINDOW

I lived in a lovely place with no noise or destruction
I lived in a land of peace
Two years later, I was older and the first house was built,
Then another and another,
Then a building plot got built,
Other buildings got built,
More got built adding another twenty-four,
All the city got too loud, so I moved away,
I was about twenty
And I went back to a quiet land.

Kevin Brady (9)
Whitdale Primary School

OUR EARTH

Birds fluttering here and there
Trees blowing softly in the air
Animals playing games with each other
Birds singing sweetly in the air
Grass gleaming in the sun
Fish swimming happily in the pond
Children playing happily on the grass
Birds and bees singing in the trees

Tractors scaring the birds and bees
Men building new buildings
Cars coming and going
No more animals or birds or bees
Roads being constructed
Trees disappearing
Birds' nests being destroyed
People walking silently

Cars driving everywhere
Skyscrapers standing big and tall
People walking loudly, people everywhere
No flowers in the city
Circus coming to town
I'm thinking of moving
No buildings, no people or the circus
Birds and bees are back again
With their little songs.

Mark Hannen (9)
Whitdale Primary School

THE VIEW FROM MY WINDOW

Grass is swaying side to side
Snow on the tree tops
Trees are shivering
Wind is blowing them
Wind is howling in a frosty, misty sky

They are building houses each day
There is nearly a city
Wind sweeping across the sky
There is a breeze on me
There are tractors

Now I am moving away
Hopefully I will be quiet again
There is no sound of cars and trucks
It will be a beautiful landscape
There are birds singing in the trees.

Lyndsay Ferrie (9)
Whitdale Primary School

THE VIEW FROM MY WINDOW

Grass is white, so is snow
Birds swoop down from trees
Cars are stuck on roads
Winds are whirling and twirling
You can see birds from my window

I can see snow
See snow drop to the ground carefully and quietly
I can see birds sing sweetly
I can see new houses being built

Birds are making nests up on trees
People on their sledges
Kids are making snowmen
People moving houses
Where it's warm and comfortable.

Ashley Black (9)
Whitdale Primary School

DESTRUCTION OF A LANDSCAPE

A land where birds swooped here and there
There the pond stood, sparkling in the sun
Butterflies fluttering in the air
Flowers bright and beautiful
In the green wilderness

Giant diggers moving and destroying
Landscape disappearing every day
Every day more houses appearing everywhere
This wilderness is disappearing

Landscape disappeared
City nearing to completion
Landscape disappeared, thinking about moving
Finally moving to a better place.

Conor MacIntyre (9)
Whitdale Primary School

THEY'RE KILLING THE FOREST

Out the window looking at lovely trees side by side
Birds flying all about, cats crying for some food
Flowers growing very tall, rabbits hopping about
Feeling happy, frogs being happy

Sale signs going up, trees getting chopped down
Birds trying to find their nests, cats and dogs crying for help
Woodland gone, children trying to play
Children getting hurt

Towns are getting built
Even big houses getting built next to my house
I think I should move away from this house now
I did . . . into a nice house.

Alexandra Paterson (9)
Whitdale Primary School

MY ENVIRONMENT

Birds tweeting very softly
Wind blowing quietly and swiftly
Animals playing gently together
Children playing in the grass
Trees blowing gently in the wind
Fish swimming in the pond
Birds swiftly flying in the sky
Grass gleaming in the sun

Tractors scare birds and bees
Men are building everywhere
Nature getting knocked down
No more animals left
Cars coming to new houses
Animals' homes getting destroyed
People running silently
Still no animals left

Circus there for children
People moving in and out
Town finished
No green land left
Animals come back
Children going to the circus
The smoke and pipes are gone
I think I will decide to move.

Stephanie Gair (9)
Whitdale Primary School

Outside My Living Room Window

Trees are swaying in the wind,
Grass shining through the fence,
Birds swooping down for food,
The wind blowing rapidly,
Hut door banging again and again.

Council chopping down the trees,
The environment is disappearing,
No trees, no forests,
Some more houses are getting built
And people are moving in.

Now the town is finished,
Children go out to play,
People walk silently on the path,
We're getting ready to move,
We've moved to another woodland
And houses are getting built again.

Kelly Johnston (9)
Whitdale Primary School

A VIEW OUT OF MY WINDOW

A beautiful garden lying in the sun
Children running in pleasure, playing tag
Berries ripening on the bush
The light breeze rustling the trees
Children yelling and playing merrily

Nature, where are you going?
Come back to where you came from
We need you to enjoy life
Building has begun
Killing everything

Sight is terrible
Horrible, even worse
Moving is the only answer
A quiet countryside
A view outside the window.

Lauren Cunningham (9)
Whitdale Primary School

OUR ENVIRONMENTAL WORLD

Our unspoilt land is shimmering with life
There are no houses to destroy the trees
Birds and the bees singing in the trees
Trees are blooming in the sun

Our landscape is turning into an urban land
Flowers die in the polluted air
Animals' houses are being destroyed
Roads are being built

Birds fluttering in the smoke
The circus is coming to town
Shops are finished in the lane
I'm thinking of moving to the countryside.

Allan Brodie (9)
Whitdale Primary School

OUTSIDE THE WINDOW

The grass is green and beautiful
The sky is blue and bright
The sun is full of light
The flowers are flowing everywhere
It's like a dream come true

The workers have started
Busy streets are near
I peer over the windowpane as if it is here
Every night I would look at the site and sigh

It's busy with traffic
There's rubbish everywhere
Dogs are roaming free
It's too busy here
I can never sleep.

Kirsty Easton (9)
Whitdale Primary School

OUTSIDE MY WINDOW

The sun is sparkling
The birds are singing
The grass is green
And the sky is blue
The flowers blow in the wind

The workers have started
The city is coming
Some houses are built
Children are running about everywhere
It's not the same now

It's busy and noisy
There are cars everywhere
Children are running free
I'm sorry we have to go
There's nothing here now.

Jade Evans (9)
Whitdale Primary School